ENDORSEMENTS

"Mark Dever introduces us to a Christian who was a faithful friend to many in his day and whose writings have instilled spiritual comfort in many more in succeeding generations, including the great preacher Martyn Lloyd-Jones. Richard Sibbes soaked strong theology in sweet love for Christ and tender mercy to broken-hearted sinners, making him a stellar example of Reformed experiential Christianity. In an age of division and discord, Sibbes strove for unity while seeking spiritual renewal in the Church of England. Dever's thorough historical research illuminates the life of this moderate Puritan, of whom it was said, 'Heaven was in him before he was in heaven.'"

—DR. JOEL R. BEEKE
President and Professor of Systematic Theology and Homiletics
Puritan Reformed Theological Seminary,
Grand Rapids, Mich.

"Richard Sibbes, once called 'the sweet dipper of grace,' is an important, but sadly neglected Puritan writer. Mark Dever's fine book helpfully puts Sibbes into context and the vitality of his theology for his day and for ours."

—DR. W. ROBERT GODFREY
President Emeritus and Professor Emeritus of Church History
Westminster Seminary California, Escondido, Calif.

"Dr. Martyn Lloyd-Jones once called Richard Sibbes 'an unfailing remedy' for the troubled of soul. Sibbes was, he wrote, 'balm to my soul at a period in my life when I was overworked and badly overtired, and therefore subject in an unusual manner to the onslaughts of the devil.' And that has been my own experience of 'the heavenly Doctor Sibbes': his heart-melting sermons seem, without fail, to draw my affections to Christ. I am delighted, then, to see this helpful and accessible introduction to Sibbes. May God use it to put many more in the way of Sibbes' rich and affecting ministry."

—Dr. Michael Reeves
President and Professor of Theology
Union School of Theology, Oxford, England

The Affectionate Theology *of*

Richard Sibbes

The Long Line of Godly Men Profiles

Series editor, Steven J. Lawson

The Expository Genius of John Calvin
by Steven J. Lawson

The Unwavering Resolve of Jonathan Edwards
by Steven J. Lawson

The Mighty Weakness of John Knox
by Douglas Bond

The Gospel Focus of Charles Spurgeon
by Steven J. Lawson

The Heroic Boldness of Martin Luther
by Steven J. Lawson

The Poetic Wonder of Isaac Watts
by Douglas Bond

The Evangelistic Zeal of George Whitefield
by Steven J. Lawson

The Trinitarian Devotion of John Owen
by Sinclair B. Ferguson

The Daring Mission of William Tyndale
by Steven J. Lawson

The Passionate Preaching of Martyn Lloyd-Jones
by Steven J. Lawson

A Long Line of Godly Men Profile

The Affectionate Theology *of*

Richard Sibbes

MARK DEVER

Reformation Trust   A DIVISION OF LIGONIER MINISTRIES, ORLANDO, FL

The Affectionate Theology of Richard Sibbes

© 2018 by Mark Dever

Published by Reformation Trust Publishing
A division of Ligonier Ministries
421 Ligonier Court, Sanford, FL 32771
Ligonier.org   ReformationTrust.com

Printed in Crawfordsville, Indiana
LSC Communications
February 2018
First edition

ISBN 978-1-56769-854-1 (Hardcover)
ISBN 978-1-56769-922-7 (ePub)
ISBN 978-1-56769-923-4 (Kindle)

Adapted from Mark E. Dever, *Richard Sibbes: Puritanism and Calvinism in Late Elizabethan and Early Stuart England* (2000).

Cover illustration: Steven Noble
Interior design and typeset: Katherine Lloyd, The DESK

Scripture quotations are from the ESV® Bible (The Holy Bible, English Standard Version®), copyright © 2001 by Crossway, a publishing ministry of Good News Publishers. Used by permission. All rights reserved.

Library of Congress Cataloging-in-Publication Data
Names: Dever, Mark, author.
Title: The affectionate theology of Richard Sibbes / Mark Dever.
Description: Orlando, FL : Reformation Trust Publishing, 2018. | Series: A long line of Godly men profile | Includes bibliographical references and index.
Identifiers: LCCN 2017036686 (print) | LCCN 2017048216 (ebook) | ISBN 9781567699227 (ePub) | ISBN 9781567699234 (Kindle) | ISBN 9781567698541
Subjects: LCSH: Sibbes, Richard, 1577-1635. | Puritans. | Theology, Doctrinal—History—17th century. | Reformed Church—Doctrines—History—17th century.
Classification: LCC BX9339.S53 (ebook) | LCC BX9339.S53 D478 2018 (print) | DDC 230/.59092--dc23
LC record available at https://lccn.loc.gov/2017036686

TABLE OF CONTENTS

Followers Worthy to Be Followed

Down through the centuries, God has raised up a long line of godly men whom He has mightily used at strategic moments in church history. These valiant individuals have come from all walks of life, from the ivy-covered halls of elite schools to the dusty back rooms of tradesmen's shops. They have arisen from all points of this world, from highly visible venues in densely populated cities to obscure hamlets in remote locations. Yet despite these diverse differences, these pivotal figures have held in common those virtues that remain nonnegotiable.

Each man possessed an unwavering faith in the Lord Jesus Christ. But more than that, each of these stalwarts of the faith held deep convictions in the God-exalting truths known as the doctrines of grace. Though they differed in secondary matters of theology, they stood shoulder to shoulder in embracing these biblical teachings that magnify the sovereign grace of God in salvation. These spiritual leaders stood upon and upheld the foundational truth that "salvation is of the Lord" (Ps. 3:8; Jonah 2:9).

Any survey of church history reveals that those who have embraced these biblical Reformed truths have been granted extraordinary confidence in their God. Far from paralyzing these spiritual giants, the doctrines of grace kindled within their hearts a reverential awe for God that humbled their souls before His throne. The truths of divine sovereignty emboldened these men to rise up and advance the cause of Christ on the earth. With an enlarged vision for the expansion of His kingdom upon the earth, they stepped forward boldly to accomplish the work of ten, even twenty men. They arose with wings like eagles and soared over their times. The doctrines of grace ignited them to serve God in their divinely appointed hour of history, leaving a godly inheritance for future generations.

This Long Line of Godly Men Profiles series highlights key figures in the agelong procession of these sovereign-grace men. The purpose of this series is to introduce you to these significant figures and explore how they used their God-given gifts and abilities to impact their times for the work of Christ. Because they were courageous followers of the Lord, their examples are worthy of our emulation today.

This volume focuses on the man who has been called "the

quintessential Puritan," Richard Sibbes. Far from embodying the misguided stereotype of the dour Puritan, Sibbes was a man on fire with passion for the gospel. Whether he was standing before the common man or before the learned man of the academy, he preached it with conviction and power. An outstanding example of a preacher who married solid Reformed theology with heartfelt zeal, Sibbes sought to unfold for his hearers the whole counsel of God in order to ensure that they understood the gospel and its implications for their lives. This doctrinally sound yet practically relevant preaching can be seen in the way he emphasized assurance of salvation, the place of emotions in Christian living, and God's covenant with man.

I want to thank the publishing team at Reformation Trust for their commitment to this Long Line of Godly Men Profiles series. I remain thankful for the ongoing influence of my former professor and revered friend, Dr. R.C. Sproul. I must also express my gratitude to Chris Larson, who is so instrumental in overseeing this series. Finally, I am grateful to Dr. Mark Dever for reworking his doctoral dissertation, *Richard Sibbes: Puritanism and Calvinism in Late Elizabethan and Early Stuart England*, in order to present this too-often-neglected figure to a new generation.

May the Lord use this book to energize and embolden a new generation of believers to bring its witness for Jesus Christ upon this world for God. Through this profile of Richard

Sibbes, may you be strengthened to walk in a manner worthy of your calling. May you be zealous in your study of the written Word of God for the exaltation of Christ and the advance of His kingdom.

Soli Deo gloria!
—Steven J. Lawson
Series editor

How This Book Came to Be

O ther than Richard Sibbes and myself, four people have been essential to the creation of this book that you're now holding. If you'll spend just a couple of minutes with me reviewing this, I think you'll better understand what this book is.

The first two people are senior scholars. William Nigel Kerr was the church history professor at Gordon-Conwell Theological Seminary in South Hamilton, Mass., who back in 1982 first suggested Richard Sibbes to me as a focus for my studies. Eamon Duffy was my supervisor in the Faculty of Divinity at the University of Cambridge, when I wrote the first edition of this book, as my dissertation (1988–92). To both men I owe a profound debt.

The third person is Michael Lawrence, a friend and colleague, who, at a turning-point in his own life, spent the better part of a year editing my dissertation for publication by Mercer University Press under the substantial title *Richard Sibbes: Puritanism and Calvinism in Late Elizabethan and Early Stuart England* (2000). Michael has since gone on to pursue his own studies at Cambridge in Thomas Goodwin, and has since 2010 been the senior pastor of Hinson Memorial Baptist Church in Portland, Ore.

And the fourth person is Kevin D. Gardner. When the idea came up of Ligonier taking my soon-to-be out-of-print dissertation on Richard Sibbes and editing it down for a more popular readership in this Long Line of Godly Men series, Kevin was assigned the task. I think that he has performed it admirably. The more obscure particulars of interest only to academics have been omitted (and can still be found in my dissertation, or in the fuller version published by Mercer). The bones of my argument are still here in my own words. We've added a little bit to make it of more general interest.

Richard Sibbes was, and is, a powerful preacher. His sermons are theologically clear and often pastorally piercing. He is another who, by grace, is in that long line of godly men.

—Mark Dever
Washington, D.C.
October 2017

The Quintessential Puritan

Someone described as "a rather bland, sweet-natured, mild-mannered, charming, learned and highly respected middle-aged gentleman" may not seem to be a promising prospect for study.[1] Though disincentives and even difficulties may discourage investigation, Richard Sibbes is an inviting subject, historically and theologically. His theology epitomizes that of the early seventeenth century under the reigns of James VI and I and Charles I, and his history illustrates conflicts and consensus within the Church of England. Even the neglect he has endured encourages investigation.

Sibbes' style of preaching—and his theology itself—were typical of the period. His sermons epitomized the practical emphasis that marked the English church at the time.

---

1   William Haller, *The Rise of Puritanism* (New York: 1938), 163.

During his life, Sibbes was recognized as an eminent, practical preacher: in 1634, Samuel Hartlib referred to him as "one of the most experimental divines now living."[2] Rarely polemical, his preaching was distinguished by its peaceable tone, more concerned with comfort than controversy. In the preface to Sibbes' *The Glorious Feast of the Gospel*, Arthur Jackson, James Nalton, and William Taylor wrote:

> Alas! Christians have lost much of their communion with Christ and his saints—the heaven upon earth— whilst they have wofully disputed away and dispirited the life of religion . . . To recover therefore thy spiritual relish of savoury practical truths, these sermons of that excellent man of God, of precious memory, are published.[3]

Later historians have realized Sibbes' ability as a preacher.[4] Yet if his ability and success were singular, his theology and aims were not.

---

2   Samuel Hartlib, *Ephemerides*, Hartlib Mss., Sheffield University.

3   Arthur Jackson, James Nalton, and William Taylor, "To the Reader," preface to *The Glorious Feast of the Gospel* by Richard Sibbes (London: 1650); repr. Alexander Balloch Grosart, ed., *The Works of Richard Sibbes*, 7 vols. (Edinburgh, Scotland: 1862–64), 2:439.

4   William Haller described Sibbes' sermons as "among the most brilliant and popular of all the utterances of the Puritan church militant" (Haller, 152). Norman Pettit suggested that Sibbes had "the richest imagination of all. Indeed, Sibbes was unique among spiritual preachers, perhaps the most original of his time" (Norman Pettit, *The Heart Prepared: Grace and Conversion in Puritan Spiritual Life* [New Haven, Conn.: 1966], 66).

Even more than his style and expression, the essence of Sibbes' theological thought was characteristic of his era, particularly in his use of the idea of covenant. Sibbes called the covenant the ground of the entirety of the Christian life "both in justification and sanctification."[5] This covenantal framework is often seen as the central difference between Calvin and his later English followers, and thus Sibbes provides a window into this uniquely English contribution. Because Sibbes' theological style and substance can be said to be both typical of and unique to the period, it is unsurprising that Christopher Hill described Sibbes as "the quintessential Puritan."[6]

Sibbes also invites study because his history illustrates agreements and conflicts within the English church at the time. His life was marked not so much by conflict and deprivation as by success in gaining positions and pulpits. From the age of ten, when he began to study at the King Edward VI Free School in Bury St. Edmunds, until his death at age 58 while preacher at Gray's Inn, London, master of Katharine Hall at Cambridge University,[7] and vicar of Holy Trinity Church, Cambridge, Sibbes was associated with well-known institutions. As such, his positions and situations act as a tour through history.

Despite his association with prominent institutions and

---

5   Sibbes, "The Rich Poverty; or, The Poor Man's Riches," in *Works*, 6:245.

6   Christopher Hill, "Francis Quarles and Edward Benlowes," in *Collected Essays* (Amherst, Mass.: 1985), 1:190.

7   The position of "master" is roughly equivalent to the American "dean." The college changed its name to St. Catherine's College in 1860.

his posthumous reputation, Sibbes has largely been neglected. Few biographies or studies of his theology exist, except for a few unpublished dissertations, and he is more often cited than studied. He provides a model for exploring and investigating "moderate Puritans," "Nonconformists," and "Calvinists." And he did not lead the life of muzzled exile that many of his contemporaries, and some friends, did. Therefore, one goal of this book is to unite the images of Sibbes' life and thought, to illuminate both him and his times.

Although a study of Richard Sibbes may prove helpful, it is not easy. Questions out-distance evidence. Difficulties, even unusual ones, abound in the study of this public man: first, Sibbes never married, so there was no obvious family member to write a biography or to collect his papers, letters, or manuscripts. Various letters and manuscripts are divided between London, Oxford, and Cambridge, but no cache of papers either by or pertaining to Sibbes exists for the historical student.

Second, and unusual in the study of a public person, is the lack of a surviving funeral sermon for him. Such sermons are important sources for the historian, as they provide contemporary insight into the subject's life. William Gouge preached Sibbes' funeral sermon, but it was never published. A brief and unsatisfying contemporary memoir of Sibbes does exist, by Zachary Catlin, and another, even shorter, published by Samuel Clarke in *A Collection of the Lives of Ten English Divines* (1652).

Besides these memoirs, the only extant sources are a few remaining letters by Sibbes; chance references in the writings of contemporaries; and the prefaces written by colleagues to his books, most of which were published posthumously. This last source points out another difficulty for the researcher—there is no record of when most of Sibbes' sermons were preached, making it difficult to reconstruct any historical progression in his thought.

A profitable study of Sibbes is still possible, however. In the first part of this book, the life of Sibbes is examined in light of his changing context. By the end of the reign of Elizabeth I in 1603, the focus of many English preachers and scholars had shifted from the controversies of the 1570s to more pastoral, less contentious concerns. Not that controversies ceased, but the literature increasingly focused on personal devotion and piety, preparation for salvation, and assurance of salvation. History has taken this literature to be typical of the loose group usually referred to as the Puritans, of which Sibbes was an acknowledged master.

This book will follow Sibbes' career and his writings, from the early years through the reign of King James and into the very different church being fashioned under King Charles I and William Laud, archbishop of Canterbury, when adherence or nonadherence to the use of the Book of Common Prayer became a primary issue (known as Conformity and Noncomformity). This book will follow Sibbes' thought by examining his theology in context: Was it distinctly Reformed? mystical?

Nonconformist? Special concern will be given to understanding how Sibbes understood the concurrence of the actions of God and the actions of humanity. This is the area in which covenant falls—and in which both the theological uniqueness of Puritanism and the distinctiveness of Sibbes' writings have usually been seen. His theology will be examined both in its most objective, Calvinistic expressions and its most "experimental," typically Puritan expressions. Especially important is his emphasis on the affections, or emotions, in the life of the Christian, as well as his insistence on the possibility of the Christian's being assured of his salvation and his exploration of the role of the conscience in the Christian life.

More generally, this book relates English Puritanism to its Reformed forefathers in a way that highlights the historical rather than the theological shifts. Therefore, Sibbes proves a useful study in the relation of Reformed theology and practice to the demands of early Stuart Conformity, and thereby in understanding the religious life of that period, when hopes for a thorough reformation were waning but had not yet mingled with desperation as fully as they would in the decade after Sibbes' death.

In the end, Sibbes will be recognized not as a moderate Puritan, forced into Nonconformity by the growing extremism of the Anglican Church under Laud, but as a Conformist to his dying day, yet one who never ceased striving for the reformation of the church.

CHAPTER ONE

Formative
Context

In the spring of 1559, a poor laborer of Pakenham, Suffolk, died, leaving behind a young wife, Elizabeth, and two sons, Paul and Robert, along with the small inheritance of a house, a little land, and a few pounds. Robert lived into his nineties, his widow Alice having no surviving children. The older son, Paul, became a wheelwright and moved to Tostock; there he married Joane, having six children who survived into adulthood.

Richard was the first of the children born to Paul and Joane Sibbes in 1577 and was baptized in the parish church on January 6, 1580. While Richard was still young, the Sibbes family moved two miles west to the town of Thurston. In his memoir of Sibbes, Zachary Catlin records that "they lived in honest repute, brought up, and married divers children, purchased some houses and lands, and there they both deceased.

His father was. . . a skilful and painful workman, and a good sound-hearted Christian."[1] There young Sibbes grew up and began his education.

All of the other Sibbes children remained in the area throughout their lives: John took up his father's trade and house in Thurston; he and his wife had a son, three grandsons, and a great-grandson who followed Richard in studying at Katharine Hall, Cambridge. John died sometime between 1610 and 1635. Thomas moved to the nearby village of Rattlesden, and married Barabara; they had no surviving offspring. The occupations of the husbands of Richard's three sisters (Susann Lopham, Elizabeth King and Margaret Mason) are unknown. Of all his siblings, only Margaret and Thomas survived Richard.

Richard did not remain in Thurston. Nevertheless, even after being elected to a fellowship at Cambridge, he did not cease to be part of his family's life in Thurston. He was prohibited from marrying—a condition of a fellowship in a Cambridge college in the seventeenth century—which perhaps increased ties to his own family. Catlin records that Sibbes would either preach in the parish church or assist him in distributing communion "whensoever he came down into

---

1   The Cambridge University Archives have three different manuscript copies of Zachary Catlin's "Memoir of Richard Sibbes" (Add. 48; Add. 103; Mm.1.49). It has been printed twice, once by J.E.B. Mayor in *Antiquarian Communications: Being Papers Presented At the Meetings of the Cambridge Antiquarian Society* (1859), 1:255–64, and once by Grosart in *The Works of Richard Sibbes* (Edinburgh, Scotland: 1862), 1:cxxxiv–cxli.

the Country, to visit his Mother and brethren"—which was frequently enough that, Catlin remarked, "wee soon grew wel acquainted."[2] Throughout his life, Sibbes held land in the village, eventually leaving it to his brother Thomas and his nephew John. Even after moving to London, Sibbes did not forget his familial responsibilities, offering to bring his mother there to live; she declined, preferring to remain in Thurston.

EARLY EDUCATION

Before his election to a Cambridge fellowship or appointment to a prominent pulpit in London, Richard's parents intended that he settle in the Thurston area and become a wheelwright like his father. While he later found in the memories of his father's work a rich store of illustrations, his own early incli-nation was to study and read.[3] So Sibbes devoted his energies instead to the labors of the academy. Catlin records:

> Testimony of Mr. Thomas Clark, High Constable, who was much of the same Age, and went to schole, together with him. . . . He hath often told me that when the Boies were dismist from Schole . . . it was

---

2   Zachary Catlin, "Memoir of Richard Sibbes," printed as "Appendix to Memoir" in *Works*, 1:cxxxv.

3   E.g., Sibbes' image of conscience as "a wedge to drive out a hard piece of wood to be cut" ("Witness of Salvation" in *Works*, 7:375), or his presenting "a man out of Christ" as "a stone out of the foundation, set lightly by, and scattered up and down here and there" ("Yea and Amen; or, Precious Promises," in *Works*, 4:123).

this Youth's constant course, as soon as he could rid himself of their unpleasing company, to take out of his Pocket or Sachel, one Book or other, and so to goe reading and meditating, til he came to his Father's house, which was neere a mile of, and so as he went to schole agen.[4]

For several years, Sibbes walked about a mile to and from the school at nearby Pakenham to be taught by Richard Brigs.[5] This was almost certainly a "petty school," an arrangement whereby a local vicar would instruct the children of his and perhaps nearby parishes in basic literacy.[6]

After attending Brigs' school, perhaps as early as 1587, Sibbes walked to the Edward VI Free School at Bury St. Edmunds, more than four miles away. It is unclear how Sibbes came to be one of the students there; statute 45 in the school's charter stated that "Poor mens children shall be received in the said school before other," yet, whether this provision would have applied to Sibbes is uncertain.[7] The educational process in the Free School was made up almost completely of

---

4   Richard Sibbes, "Judgment's Reason," in *Works*, 1:cxxxv.
5   Brigs attended St. John's, Cambridge, taking his M.A. in 1585; Pakenham was likely Brigs' first position after leaving Cambridge. He went on to become master of the Norwich Grammar School in 1598, where he remained until his death in 1636.
6   Such schools were not institutionalized and left little documentary evidence of their existence, except for references to them in historical accounts, such as Catlin's account of Sibbes. See Wrightson, 185; Barry Coward, *The Stuart Age* (London: Longman, 1980), 59.
7   See Wrightson, 189.

memorization and recitation of the Apostles' Creed, and the Lord's Prayer, the Ten Commandments in English and Latin. Through recitation they also learned Latin and Greek, reading works by Erasmus, Ovid, Cicero, Virgil, and others.[8] The regulations went so far as to require that "the scholers shall at no time depart from or out of the school to do their necessity before they have recited at their egress three several latin words, and three other at their regress."[9] The only recreation allowed was shooting arrows; when seeking an image to contrast with the judgments of God always being exactly directed, therefore, it is not surprising that Sibbes hit upon the image of God's judgment not being as "children shoot their arrows, at random."[10] They were taught from 6 a.m. until 5 p.m. on weekdays and until 3 p.m. on Saturdays and holidays.

John Wright had become schoolmaster in 1583, after a controversy resulted in the removal of the previous schoolmaster, who was suspected of being unsound in religion—probably of being a Roman Catholic. It is, therefore, likely that Wright had been carefully scrutinized by local godly gentry. The significance of this should not be lost: beginning with Sibbes' time at Bury and continuing at Cambridge, religious controversy and concern formed an important part of the context of his academic labors.

---

8   "March 12, 1583[4] Statutes of King Edward VI Free Grammar School at Bury St. Edmunds" (Suffolk County Records Office, E5/9/201.7), 22.

9   "Statutes" number 66, 16.

10   "Judgment," in *Works*, 4:78.

Throughout these years, Richard's family prospered through wheelworking, farming, and even landholding (renting houses and property in Thurston and Pakenham). Even though Paul Sibbes was a yeoman of considerable means, Richard's education was felt by his father to be financially burdensome. It was required in the statutes of the Free School in Bury that parents must pay the usher four pence "for enrolling your child's name" and provide their children with "sufficient paper, knife, pennes, bookes, candle for wynter and all other thinges at any tyme requisite and necessarie for the maynetence of his childe" including the bows and arrows for recreation.[11] Paul Sibbes' reluctance to provide for his son's education is evidenced by a remark in his will that he had been at "great charges" in Richard's education.[12]

RELIGIOUS CONTEXT

During the reigns of Henry VIII, Edward VI, and Mary I, the governance of the church was subject to violent swings between independence from and communion with Rome. Under Elizabeth I, Parliament took steps to settle the issue of

---

11 "March 12, 1583[4] Statutes of King Edward VI Free Grammar School at Bury St. Edmunds" (Suffolk County Records Office, E5/9/201.7), 25.

12 Paul Sibbes' Will, W1/67/176, Suffolk County Records Office, Bury St. Edmunds. Appendix II is a transcription of this will. Grosart, due to a misreading of Catlin's memoir, has suggested that Paul Sibbes died sometime before 1608. It is clear now from his will (drawn up in January 1610, and proved on February 15, 1610) that Paul Sibbes died in 1610 [1611].

the church's governance, resulting in what is called the Elizabethan religious settlement.

The settlement consisted two Acts of Parliament: the Act ① of Supremacy of 1558 reestablished the independence of the Church of England from Rome and recognized the British sovereign as head of the church, and the Act of Uniformity of 1559 ② mandated the use of the Book of Common Prayer in worship. Those who submitted to the acts, especially the Act of Uniformity, are called Conformists. Those who dissented, largely over aspects of the Book of Common Prayer that to some smacked of Roman Catholicism, are called Nonconformists. Many of the figures known as Puritans (so called because they wanted to purify the English church), were Nonconformists. Some remained within to church to try to encourage further reform; others, known as Separatists, later left or were ejected.

The settlement touched nearly every part of Elizabethan life. It even affected Sibbes' education. His schooling had continued because of the patronage of local men who had taken note of him.[13] In East Anglia at the time, particularly in Suffolk, it was not uncommon for preachers to exhibit some degree of Nonconformity. One such preacher was Leonard Graves, the vicar in Thurston from 1589 to 1609, who was chastised for irregular use of the surplice, a priestly garment.[14]

---

13 Wrightson, 58ff.

14 Revolt against the use of surplice was "especially notable in the archdeaconry of Suffolk," (J.F. Williams, ed., *Diocese of Norwich: Bishop Redman's Visitation*, 1597: *Presentments in the Archdeaconries of Norwich, Norfolk and Suffolk* [Norwich, England: 1946], 19).

The Elizabethan settlement was controversial, but it ushered in a time of relative religious peace in England. Nevertheless, sectarian unrest frequently bubbled under the surface and occasionally boiled over. In 1593, as the settlement entered its fourth decade, Acts of Parliament had been passed against both the Puritans and the Roman Catholics. The year 1595 saw one of the relatively few executions for heresy in Elizabeth's reign: on April 7, the Jesuit Henry Walpole was hanged as a heretic.

RELIGIOUS TURMOIL AT CAMBRIDGE

The 1590s were a time of continued religious strife in England, and the Cambridge of Sibbes' undergraduate days was not exempt from this. Cambridge was divided when it came to theological sympathies, from its leaders to its instructors, as views from staunchest Calvinism to thoroughgoing Arminianism were represented. The university Sibbes entered was a place where scholars could hear widely different understandings of the Protestant gospel. A dispute regarding predestination even led the archbishop of Canterbury, John Whitgift, to intervene in 1595. Whitgift drafted a set of theses called the Lambeth Articles, which summarized the Calvinist understanding of predestination.

In 1595, Richard Sibbes matriculated at St. John's College, Cambridge under the mastership of William Whitaker, a Calvinist who had conferred with Whitgift in the writing

[handwritten margin note: in the 1590s ?]

14

of the Lambeth Articles. St. John's had a history of ardent Protestantism, including a surreptitious meeting in the college that some had deemed a presbytery. Peter Lake wrote that "by the early 1590s St John's was divided into mutually exclusive and antagonistic groups"[15] thanks, in no small part, to Whitaker.

Soon after Sibbes' arrival, St. John's College was bereft of its master: returning to Cambridge from Lambeth on December 4, 1595, "illness supervened" and Whitaker died,[16] to be buried six days later. Within a few days, twelve of the fellows wrote to Sir William Cecil, Lord Burleigh—Elizabeth's trusted and powerful secretary—complaining of the desperate state of the college.

The election of a successor to Whitaker was a difficult one involving several candidates. In the end, Richard Clayton, master of Magdalene College and a former fellow of St. John's, was the only candidate acceptable to all sides; thus, within a month of Whitaker's death, Clayton was elected as master of St. John's College. Whitaker's successor was less sympathetic to the more radical reforming party than Whitaker was. Sibbes had entered a setting in which sermons, lectures, and conversations in the hallways must have revolved around issues of religious Conformity, with implications that went beyond simply the attire of the vicar of Thurston.

---

15 Peter Lake, *Moderate Puritans and the Elizabethan Church* (Cambridge, England: Cambridge University Press, 1982), 191.

16 Mullinger, 74.

Within the university, too, controversy continued. Peter Baro, the Lady Margaret Professor of Divinity, preached a University Sermon (at which it might reasonably be assumed Sibbes was present) in January 1596 in which he directly contradicted the Lambeth Articles. That week, he was called before some heads of houses, and the next before the consistory court. Roger Goad, provost of King's College and vice-chancellor, debated with Baro but was unsure of what to do with him. He wrote to Lord Burleigh for advice, and in his response Burleigh objected to the treatment Baro had received and even agreed with him on the disputed points. This startled the heads; after several weeks of deliberation, they replied to Burleigh, objecting to the "popery" in Baro's lectures and teaching. As the dispute widened, Baro became less certain of his position and, by autumn of Sibbes' second year, resigned his chair and fled from Cambridge. Thomas Playfere, a fellow of St. John's, was elected to succeed him.

Controversy over Calvinism continued throughout Sibbes' time at Cambridge. In 1597, William Barrett, chaplain of Gonville and Caius College and an opponent of Calvinism, fled from Cambridge to the Continent, joining the Roman Catholic Church and fulfilling fears about the consequences of his doctrinal deviations. In 1599, John Overall, master of Katharine Hall, Regius Professor of Divinity, and a critic of the Lambeth Articles, had his teaching attacked by Robert Some, master of Peterhouse.

Studies at Cambridge

By the Elizabethan period, Cambridge was recognized as being among the first rank of European universities, thrust from obscurity by the convulsions of the Reformation. Academically, Sibbes' undergraduate education would have consisted largely of the Latin and Greek classics, rhetoric, and logic. His last two years would have been rounded out by reading Aristotle, attending disputations, and giving special attention to moral, natural, and metaphysical philosophy.[17] Studying would have taken place mainly in his own chamber, his tutor's room, and in shared meetings with other students.[18] There would have been lectures to attend, with Saturday afternoons spent in catechesis in the college chapel.[19]

As an undergraduate, Sibbes was financially supported by his father with slightly more than eight pounds per year; this was supplemented with additional aid from Knewstub and Graves, and a subsizarship from the college.[20] As a sizar, Sibbes again experienced the benefits of patronage: sizars were "men who only indirectly benefited by college endowments to the

---

17 For more on the typical course of B.A. studies for a Cambridge undergraduate of the period, see John Twigg, *A History of Queens' College, Cambridge 1448–1986* (Cambridge, England: Boydell, 1987), 98.

18 Twigg, 94.

19 See "An. 1588. Maii 17. A Decree, by Will. Whitaker, Master, and the seniors," printed in *Reports from the Select Committees: Education of the Lower Orders* (London: 1818), 4:405.

20 "Caitlin Memoir," in *Works*, 1:xxxxv.

extent of, perhaps, receiving rooms and tuition free, but were attached to a Fellow or Fellow Commoner of the College who in return for some kind of service provided them with funds for maintenance, the service and help being undefined."[21]

In a sermon, Sibbes noted that some words in Romans 11 "should stir us up earnestly to take our part in that Christ hath provided, because we know not how soon the table will be taken away. When men see the dishes in removing, though before they have discoursed away much time of their supper, yet then they will fall fresh to it."[22] This scene of men rushing to finish their supper was one that would have naturally been in Sibbes' mind as one who had eaten in common halls almost all his adult life. During his time at Cambridge, one duty he certainly would have performed would have been waiting at tables; others were probably menial chores assigned at his fellow's discretion. This is not to suggest that sizarships were demeaning positions; often they were the primary means of financial support for students who could not otherwise afford an education. Whatever the nature of Sibbes' sizarship, it was sufficient to see him through his first degree.

By the time Sibbes graduated from St. John's College in 1599, England was changing. The same year saw Burleigh, a friend of moderate reform in the nation, church, and university, die. With Burleigh's death, and the deaths of Elizabeth

---

21 R.F. Scott, "Some Aspects of College Life in Past Times" in *The Eagle*, 162; repr. in Scott, *Notes from the Records of St. John's College, Cambridge*, 4th series (privately printed: 1913–34), item XI. Cf. Twigg, 89ff.

22 "Bowels Opened," in *Works*, 2:35.

and Whitgift in the following years, those who had held together the Elizabethan settlement more than any others for the previous four decades passed from the scene.

But this was after Sibbes' initial period in Cambridge. During his first years as a student, the Lambeth Articles, though they were later largely disregarded, created the climate of a clear soteriological Calvinism that the Church of England and the universities espoused and taught. No doubt Sibbes' future Conformity was influenced by the patronage he had enjoyed and the controversies he had observed while a student at St. John's.

CHAPTER TWO

Sibbes and Conformity

Within two weeks of the death of Elizabeth I, James VI of Scotland journeyed south from Edinburgh to ascend to the throne of England as James I. Heir to the English throne through his great-grandmother Margaret Tudor (the sister of Elizabeth's father, Henry VIII), James met with great anticipation and fanfare along with the way owing to the nation's relief at an orderly and peaceful succession.

On his way in April 1603, James was made aware of one area of discontent in his new kingdom—its religious life—by the presentation of the Millenary Petition.[1] A group of Puritans drafted the petition to present the new king with their grievances regarding the state of the Anglican Church. James heard their complaints at the Hampton Court Conference in

---

1   Reprinted in J.P. Kenyon, *The Stuart Constitution: Documents and Commentary*, 2nd ed. (Cambridge, England: Cambridge University Press, 1986), 117–19.

January 1604 and later said that he had been "impressed by the puritans as agitators and conspirators . . . but not with the gravity of their demands. The more moderate, even trivial, their case, the less excuse for disturbing the peace and unity of the church."[2]

Having attended to the Puritans' complaints, James expected adherence to the law of the church as expressed in the recently formulated Canons of 1604. The particular cause of "so much broyle in the Church and hart burninge"[3] were the three articles of canon 36, which affirmed the ecclesiastical supremacy of the king in England and asserted that the Book of Common Prayer and the present structure of the Church of England were not contrary to the Word of God, that the king himself "will use the form of the said book prescribed in public prayer and administration of the sacraments, and none other," and that the Thirty-Nine Articles were biblical.

The canons required subscription, in the form of a signature. In restating the terms of the Acts of Supremacy and Uniformity, the Canons of 1604 became the new standard for Conformity. Failure to conform, even after subscription, was ground for suspension and, "if obstinate," excommunication.[4]

---

2   Patrick Collinson, "The Jacobean Religious Settlement: The Hampton Court Conference," in *Before the English Civil War*, ed. Howard Tomlinson (London: Palgrave, 1983), 44. Cf. Kenneth Fincham and Peter Lake, "The Ecclesiastical Policy of King James I," *Journal of British Studies* (April 1985): 24:171.

3   Stephen Egerton, "Address to Convocation, urging a revision of the newe booke of common prayer," cited in S.B. Babbage, *Puritanism and Richard Bancroft* (London: SPCK, 1962), 79.

4   Canon 38.

The campaign for Conformity that followed "proved to be the end of the puritan movement in the form of a concerted effort mounted from within the Church to alter the fundamental terms of the Elizabethan settlement by political means."[5]

There were other ways of achieving reforms in the church, including the training of young ministers in the universities. A former Cambridge fellow, reflecting on the leading role of his alma mater, wrote that "Cambridge is or should be, as an eye to all our land: so that the alterations that fall out there cannot but bee felt of all parts."[6] Yet Cambridge changed along with the national church. The Earl of Essex was succeeded as chancellor by Sir Robert Cecil, who, if not less Protestant, was at least more fully the Queen's tool than Essex had been. The deaths of the leading Puritan theologians William Perkins (1602) and Thomas Cartwright (1603) were further signs of the changing church. More alarming was the new king's reference to the church of Rome as a "true, but corrupt church" in the opening speech to his first Parliament on March 19, 1604.

Even as the changing bounds of Conformity fell across many godly consciences, they also enlarged to embrace many

---

5   Collinson, "Jacobean," 45. Cf. Patrick Collinson, *The Elizabethan Puritan Movement* (London: Oxford University Press, 1967), 448–67; Peter Clarke, "Josiah Nichols and religious radicalism 1553–1639," *Journal of Ecclesiastical History* (April 1977), XXVIII/2:145–50.

6   William Ames(?), preface to Paul Baynes, *The Diocesans Triall* (London: 1621), 2. Cf. Rosemary O'Day, *The English Clergy: The Emergence and Consolidation of a Profession 1558–1642* (Leicester, England: 1979), 138–42; Charles Carlton, *Archbishop William Laud* (London: Routledge & Kegan Paul, 1987), 138; Victor Morgan, "Cambridge University and "The Country' 1560–1640" in *The University in Society*, Lawrence Stone, ed. (London: Oxford University Press, 1975), 1:225–43.

whose opinions previously would have been considered beyond the pale in a Reformed church. In 1605, Bishop William Chaderton of Lincoln was pressured into silencing Arthur Hildersham for Nonconformity. Five years later, Nicholas Rushe was ordered by the vice-chancellor's court to disavow an offensively Puritan sermon he had preached, and—when he refused—expelled from the college and the university. Such was the flavor of the Early Stuart church, and the shifts of the national church were felt in Cambridge.

POSITIONS AT CAMBRIDGE

Sibbes, however, had been in Cambridge for ten years before James ascended the throne. The Cambridge Sibbes first knew was the late–Elizabethan Cambridge, with Burleigh as chancellor, and had been excited by William Whitaker, William Perkins, William Ames, Paul Baynes, and Robert Some. By the time of James' ascension, Sibbes had earned his B.A. and M.A., after being one of nine admitted as Foundress Fellows of St. John's, for his native county of Suffolk. While being made a fellow was the mark of a good college career in early seventeenth century, it was perhaps also an indication of no other immediate prospects.

At the same time, it appears that Sibbes was an engaged and successful fellow, serving in a variety of posts in college, including several chaplaincy positions.[7] From these positions,

---

7 The record of Sibbes' positions in college are to be found not primarily in the college registers, but in the college rental books for 1600–1618 (SJCArchives SB4.3)

Sibbes merely drew extra income and perhaps had regular duties in chapel, yet it was an honor, because of the limited number of chaplaincies in the college. As a sublector in 1603, Sibbes' main duty would have been to assist the principal and (other) lectors in the morning with practical arrangements, perhaps substituting for them sometimes. As an examiner for four years, Sibbes would have been questioned undergraduates daily on the lectures in the subjects of rhetoric (classics), dialectics (logic), mathematics, or philosophy. St. John's, for Sibbes, was a training ground in Reformed divinity, and that exercised with politic restraint.

By his final years of residency, Sibbes was elected to three of the most important posts in the college: in the year 1615, both senior dean and lector domesticus of the college[8] and, as senior dean, would have been the final authority in the administration (other than the master and seniors) of all aspects of the students' lives from matriculation to commencement, including their religious, academic, moral, and social lives. The position of lector domesticus is less well understood, but is perhaps to be identified with the position of principal lector of the college. If that is the case, Sibbes would also have delivered lectures throughout the week on various subjects. Such positions not only brought Sibbes into more intimate contact with the running of his own college but also gave him

---

and for 1619–33 (SJCArchives SB4.4). Almost all of these offices were by annual election of the master and seniors.

8 Baker referred to the offices of lector and dean as usually falling "upon men of learning," as the other offices (e.g. bursar) "fell upon men of business" (Baker, 1:206).

opportunity to interact with prominent visitors—including the king himself.

In 1617, Sibbes left for London to take the position of preacher at Gray's Inn, one of England's legal professional associations. Still, he maintained ties to Cambridge, and in 1619 was elected senior fellow of St. John's College, a position that, with the master of the college and the other senior fellows, exercised power over college matters.[9] The senior fellows, virtually in tandem with the master, had a share in the dividends of the college—about eight times larger than the share of the junior fellows. Knowledge of Sibbes' positions at St. John's helps explain his later election as master of Katharine Hall, Cambridge; given the other posts he had held, being a senior fellow of St. John's would have naturally suggested Sibbes as a likely master of a college.

In the larger sphere of university life, Sibbes served as taxor for the university in 1608, with the responsibility of seeing that just weights and measures were used by the town merchants in the selling of goods to the students. It was usually a position held by someone making the university his career; by this and by being ordained, Sibbes had risen in social status, becoming a member of the gentry. Thus, Sibbes evidenced the rapid social change typical of late Elizabethan and early Stuart England.[10] His grandfather had been merely a laborer,

---

9   On the Statutes of 1580, see James B. Mullinger, *St. John's College* (London: 1901), 67–71. Cf. Miller, 29–34.

10   Keith Wrightson, *English Society 1580–1680* (London: Routeledge, 1982), 17–38.

his father a yeoman; Richard Sibbes was a gentleman—or at least an academic.

CONVERSION

However, Cambridge was, for Sibbes, not only a place for career, but also for conversion. Elizabethan Cambridge offered much to commend a serious contemplation of religion, from regular sermons to monthly communion, required prayers to outbreaks of the plague. At some point, probably soon after he became a fellow, Sibbes was "changed": "It pleased God to convert him by the Ministry of Master Paul Baines, whilest he was Lecturer at Saint Andrews in Cambridge."[11] Baynes was, as Sibbes described after his death, "of a sharp wit, and clear judgment: though his meditations were of a higher strain than ordinary, yet he had a good dexterity, furthered by his love to do good, in explaining dark points with lightsome similitudes."[12] Sibbes later wrote, "As the minister speaks to the ear, Christ speaks, opens, and unlocks the heart at the same time; and gives it power to open, not from itself, but

---

11 Samuel Clarke, "The life of Doctor Sibs," in *A general martyrologie, containing a collection of all the greatest persecutions which have befallen the church of Christ . . . Whereunto is added the lives of thirty-two English Divines*, 3rd ed. (London: 1677), 143. This is the only contemporary statement about Sibbes' own conversion.

12 Sibbes, "To the Reader" in Paul Baynes, *A Commentary Upon the First Chapter of the Epistle . . . to the Ephesians*, repr. in *Works*, 1:lxxxv. See also Keith Sprunger, *The Learned Doctor William Ames: Dutch Backgrounds of English and American Puritanism* (Urbana, Ill.: University of Illinois Press, 1972), 37, 192–93.

from Christ."[13] There is no evidence that this conversion was dramatic; in fact, Sibbes' lack of allusion to his own conversion, and repeated references to its gradual nature, may reflect that he was one whom he described as "those who have kept themselves from the common pollutions and gross sins of the time. It pleaseth God that faith comes upon them, though they know not how for the time."[14]

On February 21, 1608, Sibbes was ordained as a deacon and a priest in the Church of England, at age 30. Why he waited for more than six years after reaching the canonical age for ordination is unclear. One reason would have been that he did not consider himself converted until sometime after 1602. If he did present papers of testimony from "credible" people who had known his life and behavior for three years previous (as some were asked to do, according to canon 34), he may have wanted to wait for three years beyond his conversion—suggesting that it occurred in 1605. The rush of college business and academic life could also have prevented him from either deciding to seek ordination, or from seeking it once he had decided. Though being ordained as a deacon and a priest on the same day was officially prohibited (as were ordinations outside of the Sundays following an Ember week), it was a common practice—in fact, Sibbes was ordained with eight other young men that day and was not the only one to receive both simultaneously.

---

13 "Bowels Opened," in *Works*, 2:63; cf. "Fountain," in *Works*, 5:469.
14 "Witness," in *Works*, 7:375–76.

Once ordained, Sibbes quickly gained a reputation as a good preacher among the people of Cambridge.[15] He would have had opportunities to preach or lecture in town or nearby country churches.[16] The records of St. John's state that Sibbes was elected as a college preacher on March 1, 1609, and that he continued to serve in this capacity throughout his time as a fellow.[17] Since his preaching could not have begun before February 1608, it seems certain that Sibbes' reputation arose primarily through these sermons delivered in the college chapel.

The year 1610 saw Sibbes recognized by both the university and the town of Cambridge. He was granted the bachelor of divinity, which required that he preach one public sermon in English and one in Latin to the university, answer questions put to him by members of the university on two points of divinity for two hours, and, reply against someone else on two different topics, on separate days in the same place; all the above activities taking place within one year.[18] He was also selected to be the "responder" at the commencement exercises, at which he defended two beliefs common to the moderate Puritans of the day.

---

15 "Caitlin Memoir," in *Works*, 1:xxxxv.

16 One of William Whitaker's complaints twenty years earlier, against another fellow of St. John's, Everard Digby, had been that "he never preacheth any sermons more than of necessity he must neither at Cambridge nor else where for anything we know." Letter of William Whitaker to Lord Burleigh, dated 26 October 1590, St. John's College Library.

17 St. John's College Archives SB4.4.

18 William Harrison, *The Description of England*, ed. G. Edelen (Ithaca, N.Y.: 1968), 73.

The second recognition, and one far more significant in shaping historians' perceptions of Sibbes, came from the town. The minister, church wardens, and twenty-nine other parishioners of Holy Trinity Church established a lecture series by popular subscription. On November 22, they wrote to Richard Sibbes as follows:

> To Mr. Sibs publique pracher of the Towne of Cambridge. We whose names ar heer Underwritten the Churchwardens and parishioners of Trinity parishe in Cambridge, with the ful & fre consent of Mr. John Wildbore our minister, duely considering the extream straytnes & divers other discomodities concerning the accustomed place of your exercises, & desireing as much as in us lyeth the more publique benefit of your ministry, doe earnestly entreat you wold be pleased to accept of our parishe churche, which al of us doe willinglye offer you for & concerning the exercising of your ministery & awditorye at the awntient and usual daye & howre. In witness hereof we have heerunto set to our hands this 22nd of November 1610.
>
> Joh. Wilbore, Minister.
> Edward Almond,
> Thomas Bankes, Churchewardens
> [Signed also by 29 Parishioners.][19]

19   C.H. Cooper, *Annals of Cambridge* (Cambridge, England: 1845) 3:229.

Sibbes is called "publique p'cher of the Towne of Cambridge," not as a reference to his having held a public lectureship previous to this one,[20] but in that he was a public preacher (i.e., a preacher in English, rather than Latin) in the town of Cambridge. The mention of "the extream straytnes & div'se other discomodities concerning the accustomed place of your exercises, & desireing as much as in us lyeth the more publique benefit of yor ministry" is intriguing; it seems clear from the decree for "publick sermons" that the "accustomed place of your exercise" was the chapel at St. John's. It is unsurprising that townsmen would consider a college chapel discommodious, as its small size and seating arrangement would have been less than ideal for a popular lecture. Whether there or elsewhere, it was a place that at least these parishioners considered less convenient than Holy Trinity would be. The "awntient and usuall day and hour" were Sundays at one o'clock in the afternoon, the same time as the university lecture at Great St. Mary's and, more significantly, the same time at which these townspeople had likely heard Sibbes preach "publick sermons" at St. John's chapel. For his troubles, Sibbes' was to be paid 40 pounds per year, raised by public subscription.

---

20 As J. Barton suggested in "Notes on the Past History of the Church of Holy Trinity, Cambridge," *Cambridge Antiquarian Society Communications* (Cambridge, England: 1869–70), 4:319.

DOUBLY DEPRIVED AT CAMBRIDGE?

The picture of Sibbes that comes to us is of an early Stuart preacher who neither approved of nor practiced kneeling in communion, wearing the surplice, or signing the cross in baptism, yet who remained within the established church. He is presented as a respected yet persecuted minister, one who was deprived of two positions, censured, and silenced. Thus, Sibbes became a model for numerous disciples who would later dissent from the Church of England. It has been supposed that only the power of his lawyer friends and noble patrons allowed him to retain his later ministry at Gray's Inn for almost two decades.

After his death, his writings became almost entirely the possession of Nonconformists, and Sibbes came to be read through Separatist spectacles. Although he was remembered as espousing a robustly Reformed theology, it was his moderation that was particularly admired by those who followed him. Sibbes stood above the tumult of the times, "to preserve the vitals and essentials of religion, that the souls of his heareres, being captivated with the inward beauty and glory of Christ, and being led into an experimental knowledge of heavenly truths, their spirits might not evaporate and discharge themselves in endless, gainless, soul-unedifying, and conscience perplexing questions."[21] So the perception of Sibbes has remained—a

---

21 Simeon Ash, James Nalton and Joseph Church, "To the Reader" in Sibbes, *A Heavenly Conference Between Christ and Mary after His Resurrection* (London: 1654); repr. in *Works*, 6:415.

paradox of tumultuous, conflict-filled career and arrestingly "sweet," gentle writings.

In his introduction to Sibbes' *The Glorious Feast of the Gospel*, Arthur Jackson wrote that "we need say nothing of the author . . . his memory is highly honoured amongst the godly-learned."[22] The celebrity that had come to Richard Sibbes by 1650 was heightened by the memory of his conflict and suffering to remain both godly and conforming. With Laud as his antagonist, Sibbes was included among a group of eminent theologians who were "brought into the High Commission and troubled or silenced for a time, by his [Laud's] procurement upon frivolous pretences: But in truth, because they were principle Props of our Protestant Religion, against his Popish and Arminian Innovations."[23] Laud did harass Sibbes once in London, for his involvement in circulating a letter that was deemed politically inexpedient and for involvement as a leader in the Feoffees for Impropriations, an organization of Puritans.

But the picture of the harassed Sibbes went beyond even that, reaching back into his days in Cambridge. Sibbes was described in Thomas Ball's biography of John Preston as having found refuge at Gray's Inn after being "outed both of fellowship & Lecture in the university."[24]

---

22 Arthur Jackson, James Nalton and William Taylor, "To the Reader" in Sibbes, *The Glorious Feast of the Gospel* (London: 1650); repr. in *Works*, 2:442.

23 William Prynne, *Canterburies Doome* (London: 1646), 362.

24 Thomas Ball, "Life of the Renowned Doctor [John] Preston," quoted in Clarke, *A general martyrologie*, 108.

Was Sibbes really outed? In neither of Sibbes' memoirs, nor in any of the introductions to thirty posthumously published volumes of his works, are these two deprivations mentioned. Zachary Catlin's memoir of Sibbes, written at the request of Sir William Spring in 1652, omitted any reference to Sibbes' lectureship at Holy Trinity church. The other contemporary memoir of Sibbes was by Samuel Clarke—"The Life of Doctor Sibs"—published in *A general martyrologie* (1652). This brief work was based upon Clarke's own knowledge, information gleaned from introductions to Sibbes' works, and conversation with William Gouge—a particularly important source who, as a friend of Sibbes and the preacher of Sibbes' funeral sermon, would have known of any deprivations Sibbes suffered, especially if they caused his removal from Cambridge to London.[25] Yet, Clarke made no allusion to Sibbes' Cambridge deprivations, even after he had edited in the previous year the life of Preston, in which both deprivations were mentioned.

In fact, no seventeenth-century memoir of Sibbes recorded any such deprivations; the only accounts of them were as an aside in a memoir of John Preston, written as late as 1650. Is it likely that this additional information reflected more accurate knowledge of Sibbes by Ball than Catlin or Clarke had? Or, do the silences of Catlin and Clarke bring into question the accuracy of Ball's description? That Ball's information was more accurate than the others seems doubtful: Ball was

---

25 Clarke, in *A general martyrologie*, 144, mentions having spoken with Gouge about Sibbes.

in Cambridge as an undergraduate during the final year and a half of Sibbes' lectureship at Holy Trinity and would have known of Sibbes' departure to London. Catlin was a personal friend of Sibbes, and it would be surprising for these deprivations to be omitted. Clarke, however, would have known about such deprivations had they occurred. Thus, from these considerations alone, one might wonder whether Sibbes' deprivations actually occurred.

Sibbes was not deprived of his fellowship at St. John's in 1615. We have already noted Sibbes' election as a senior fellow of the College in 1619. His quarterly payments from the college as a college preacher and commons and livery allowances continued into 1626 as well.

The question of his having been "outed" from the lectureship is more ambiguous. It is certain that he was asked to begin the lecture at Holy Trinity in November 1610, and that he was chosen preacher of Gray's Inn, London, in February 1617—but there is no reason for accepting that he was deprived of this lecture in the year 1615. That date was suggested due to a misreading of a statement, based on an assumption, based on a mistake.

The 1615 date[26] for the suppression of the Holy Trinity lecture is called into question by an instrument for the construction of a new gallery in the church, which is dated March 4, 1615,[27] and made almost impossible by an edict of

---

26 Or early 1616, as Grosart would have it.

27 Cambridge Shire Hall, Parish Records, P22/6.2.

King James (that almost certainly was issued on December 3, 1616), when James met with the heads of Cambridge houses to discuss ecclesiastical matters in the university. Their conversation matches almost exactly the written edict,[28] which does not seem to include a suppression of the lecture at Holy Trinity, but only forbid lectures which conflicted with the catechizing in the colleges[29]—and since the lecture at Holy Trinity was held at 1 p.m., it was not affected by the edict.[30] James had apparently expressed his desire that students should attend the university lecture at Great St. Mary's rather than others, but this was only directed to the students and was not repeated in the written directions given to the heads.[31]

A memorandum dated December 6, 1616, records Sibbes' subscription, with some questions and hesitation, to the three problematic articles of the Canons of 1604. He voiced some concern with making the sign of the cross, which he said was dangerous, though not contrary to the Word of God

---

28 Public Records Office, State Papers Domestic, James I, SP14/89, f.113–14. Cf. James' "Memorial" of twelve years earlier (State Papers Domestic, James I, SP10/68).

29 An exercise that was done from 3 to 4 p.m. on Sundays.

30 See CUA Mm.1.38, 137, for a reference in a letter from Viscount Dorchester to Vice-Chancellor Butts dated May 11, 1630, about the lectureship at Holy Trinity, in which Dorchester mentioned that the lecture had "for many yeares past . . . been held at one of the clocke in the afternoon . . ." the same time as the University Lecture in Great St. Mary's. This letter has been reprinted in Cooper, 3:229–30.

31 Is this also the occasion to which Thomas Ball referred in his memoir of John Preston: "About that time the lecture at Trinity-church, and the sermons at St Andrews, were prohibited, and the scholars all confined to St Mary's. . . ."? Thomas Ball, *The Life of the Renowned Doctor Preston*, E.W. Harcourt, ed. (Oxford, England: 1885), 42–43.

and thus allowable. [32] An account from the next day records Sibbes' apparent concern that some might misunderstand the sign of the cross in baptism. This account again notes that Sibbes subscribed to the canons. [33]

That Sibbes was even asked to conform, and that he was referred to as a "town preacher," proves that Sibbes was still lecturing at Holy Trinity in December 1616. Less than two months later, he was chosen as preacher of Gray's Inn, London. While it is possible that Sibbes was deprived later in December or January, it seems unlikely; no evidence for it exists beyond Ball's mention. It appears, therefore, that Sibbes was deprived neither of his fellowship nor of his lectureship.

The modern historian can only guess why would Ball have reported these deprivations or supposed them to have occurred.[34] Perhaps he had heard that Sibbes was called in to subscribe, that there were questions about the matter, and that soon afterward he left for London. That might plausibly explain Ball's references to Sibbes as having been "outed both of fellowship & Lecture in the university," which became

---

32 CUA Vice Chancellor's Court I.42. f. 202. See Victor Morgan's reporting of this incident in his "Country, Court and Cambridge University: 1558–1640: A Study in the Evolution of a Political Culture" (Ph.D. diss., University of East Anglia: 1983), 2:208.

33 CUALett. 11.A.A.8.d.

34 Ball's memoir is not altogether accurate in other respects. For example, he said that Preston was elected preacher of Lincoln's Inn, London in 1622, when that post fell vacant by John Donne's death; Donne, however, did not die until 1631. Cf. Irvonwy Morgan, *Prince Charles's Puritan Chaplain* (London: Allen and Unwin, 1957), 117–24.

the basis for remaking this otherwise moderate Puritan into a Nonconformist.[35]

Ironically, all of this led to a very different impression of Sibbes than one would gather from his writings and from reading about his character and temperament from his contemporaries. The fact that Sibbes did subscribe in December 1616 disproves the idea that he was an open Nonconformist—a hesitater, yes, and a questioner; but not a Dissenter. Yet with these deprivations removed from the foreground, the conciliating tone of his writings appears more consistent with his own person, and his later preferments become more understandable. The picture of Sibbes—as a Reformer, but a cautious one; as a Puritan, but a moderate one—is consistent with the rest of Sibbes' life and activities in Cambridge and London.[36]

THE COMMUNION OF SAINTS

One of the most striking aspects of Richard Sibbes' sermons is his frequent and powerful reference to friendship. "What

---

35 While there is no certain date for the composition of Ball's life of Preston, it seems to have been composed sometime well after Preston's death in 1628; perhaps it was written for Clarke's "lives of sundry modern divines," where it first appeared in 1651 (Samuel Clarke, *A general martyrologie. . .Whereunto are added the lives of sundry modern divines* [London: 1651]). The mistaken date for John Donne's death, the reference to "very many yet alive" which can witness to Preston's manner of life, the reference to Henry Yelverton's and Sibbes' death, and the explanation of what the obligations of Charles' royal chaplains were, all show that the composition was well removed from 1628.

36 For a fuller treatment of Sibbes focusing on the question of his having been deprived of his lectureship at Holy Trinity Church and his fellowship at St. John's College, see this author's "Moderation and Deprivation: A Re-appraisal of Richard Sibbes," *Journal of Ecclesiastical History* (July 1992): 43:396–413.

makes the life of man comfortable? There is a presence of God in meat, in drink, in friends."[37] In his treatment of Psalm 42:11, he delivered one of the most beautiful and passionate sections of these sermons, in what amounts to a verbal rhapsody on friendship:[38]

> There is a sweet sight of God in the face of a friend; for though the comfort given by God's messengers be ordinarily most effectual, as the blessing of parents, who are in God's room, is more effectual than the blessing of others upon their children, yet God hath promised a blessing to the offices of communion of saints performed by one private man towards another.[39]

Godly friends were walking sermons.[40] Sibbes described God himself as "the great Friend,"[41] and Christ was characterized by "a winning, gaining disposition," which was to be in his followers.[42] Sibbes proved to have such a nature: By 1624, his ministry in London had been so well-received at Gray's

---

37 Sibbes, "A Breathing after God" in *Works*, 2:228–29.

38 Sibbes, "The Soul's Conflict with Itself" in *Works*, 1:191–93; cf. "Bowels Opened," in *Works*, 2:36–37; "Excellency," 4:262.

39 "Soul's Conflict," in *Works*, 1:192; cf. ibid., 1:191.

40 Sibbes, "The Bride's Longing," in *Works*, 6:560; cf. Sibbes' "Angels' Acclamations" in *Works*, 6:321; "Pattern," in *Works*, 7:515; "Rich Poverty," in *Works*, 6:237; "Soul's Conflict," in *Works*, 1:192.

41 "Saint's Hiding-Place," in *Works*, 1:411; cf. "Bowels Opened," in *Works*, 2:37.

42 "Excellency," in *Works*, 4:262; cf. "The Bruised Reed and Smoking Flax," in *Works*, 1:51.

Inn that, just as at Holy Trinity Church, the auditorium had to be enlarged. As one somewhat estranged from his father, removed from his family, and unmarried, Sibbes could well appreciate the value of friendships.

Furthermore, the communion of saints was readily available to Sibbes throughout his life. He had risen by friends, and the places to which he rose required friendships to be important. From a young age, Sibbes was not only a bachelor, but lived in communities of bachelors—St. John's, Gray's Inn, Katharine Hall.[43] A person in his position might well have found himself never more than once or twice removed from a great part of the university-educated clergy of the time, and from the greater part of the political and financial nation.

Sibbes clearly had an extensive tree of friendships throughout the London legal, merchant, and clergy communities and beyond. This is hardly surprising, given that Sibbes was primarily a preacher and a pastor. Reflecting on Sibbes' successful mastership at Katharine Hall, W.H.S. Jones wrote that he was "an able, pious man, with a gift of making friends."[44] His skill as a preacher proved pivotal in these relationships: Sibbes' lectures brought him to the attention of other fellows, students, ministers, and patrons in Cambridge, and probably brought him to London; were it not for his preaching, there is no apparent reason why Sibbes might not have continued

---

43 Gray's Inn required its lecturer to be unmarried. See Reginald Fletcher, ed., *The Pension Book of Gray's Inn . . . 1569–1669* (London: 1901), 139; cf. 224.

44 W.H.S. Jones, *A History of St. Catharine's College* (Cambridge, England: 1936), 92.

on as a fellow of St. John's until his death. Once in London, it was primarily through his lectures there that he came to the attention of the godly throughout the city and the country. From there, Sibbes became one of the most important links between the godly lawyers and the godly ministers in London.

Taken together, Sibbes' connections through the Inns of Court (the legal societies) brought him close friendships with an impressive array of Parliamentary leaders of the early Stuart era. Whether listening to him preach, working for his promotion, cooperating with him at Gray's Inn, sponsoring godly preaching, or agitating for the concerns of the godly in the House of Commons, these men supported and encouraged Sibbes in his ministry. Sibbes preached from experience when he said, "Men willingly look upon examples. The examples of great and excellent persons; the example of loving and bountiful persons; the example of such as are loving and bountiful to us in particular; the example of such as we have interest in, that are near and dear to us, and we to them—these four things commend examples."[45]

Reflection upon the evidence suggests that among his closest friends seem to have been: fellow Cantabrigians and London ministers William Gouge and John Preston; among the lawyers and Parliamentarians, John Pym and Sir Nathaniel Rich; and among other patrons, Mrs. Mary More, Lady Elizabeth Brooke, and Robert Rich, Earl of Warwick. All were

---

45 "Church's Riches," in *Works*, 4:520.

remembered in Sibbes' will (except Preston, who predeceased him, and Warwick); all clearly shared Sibbes' zeal for godly preaching. And none, during Sibbes' lifetime, countenanced separation from the Church of England.

This last point is important. During the time that Sibbes knew these people, they were cautious: matters of principle were not to be compromised; yet the established form of government in the English church called for no compromise of principles in and of itself. It was not seen to be at fault—rather, its working in certain particular instances was misguided. Sibbes had seen the dangers of even merely perceived radical dissent and had learned that the system was best changed, if at all, only slightly and from within.

CHAPTER THREE

The Contentious Age

In the seventeenth century, "change" would likely have suggested decline or decay.[1] "Changes" would have been not progress, but "falls"—whether of Adam and Eve, or of Rome.[2] There was a desire to imitate classical styles in writing, and idealization of the Anglo-Saxon past was popular. Even the introduction of the widespread use of the coach was seen not as part of the inevitable evolution of transport but rather as a new irritation that gutted the streets of London, making them far more dangerous for most. Heaven would be a place where man would be "altogether unchangeable,"[3] for changes

---

1   "Fountain Opened," in *Works*, 5:512. Cf. J.T. Cliffe, *The Puritan Gentry: The Great Puritan Families of Early Stuart England* (London: Routledge & Kegan Paul, 1984), 59; Johann Summerville, "Ideology, Property and the Constitution," in *Conflict in Early Stuart England*, eds. R. Cust and A. Hughes (London: Routledge, 1989), 62.

2   "Fountain Opened," in *Works*, 5: 466.

3   "Bowels Opened," in *Works*, 2:37–38; and "Soul's Conflict," in *Works*, 1:282.

by man were "innovations"—a powerful polemical tool for those in the church decrying change in religion.[4]

The status quo was thought to be fundamentally correct. The fact that Richard Sibbes appeared to share in this conception may account for the uncontroversial nature of much of Sibbes' preaching—yet to see Sibbes as a Puritan mystic detached from history is to ignore the import of his words in their time. A careful reading of his sermons reveals more interaction with opponents than one might at first suppose from so pacific a divine. That such statements do not appear more often may have been due to Sibbes' wariness of offending those in authority, perhaps altering what had been preached to make it more acceptable before publication. Therefore, the apparent "timelessness" in Sibbes' sermons reflects, in part, the perils of his times. His moderation was not a pious apathy, but more akin to the proper balance of humors in the body, which would ensure the health of his patient; it was a selective mixture of conservatism and further reform. Therefore, to better understand Sibbes' moderation, his work and preaching must be seen in the mixture of those things that he would defend and those he would not.

---

4   See "Fountain Opened," in *Works*, 5:466, 511; "Excellency," in *Works*, 4:241; "Divine Meditations," in *Works*, 7:223; "Judgment," in *Works*, 4:95, 101; "The Saint's Safety in Evil Times, Manifested by St. Paul, From his Experience of God's Goodness in Greatest Distress," in *Works*, 1:301. Cf. "Excellency," in *Works*, 4:303; "Proclamation for the establishing of the peace and quiet of the Church of England," repr. in Kenyon, *The Stuart Constitution*, 138–39; and "The King's Declaration," reprinted S.R. Gardiner, *Constitutional Documents of the Puritan Revolution*, 3rd ed. (Oxford, England: 1906), 77–82, 89.

INNOVATIONS IN IMMODERATE TIMES

Sibbes came to London as the newly elected divinity lecturer for Gray's Inn; as such, he was to be unmarried, having no other cure of souls, and was to provide two lectures each Sunday in the chapel for members of the inn. In return, he was given a generous salary, chambers in the inn, and money for board during vacations.[5] The position had fallen open on January 16, 1616, when Roger Fenton died. At an unusually well-attended meeting of the Pensioners on February 5, 1617, Sibbes was elected.[6] Though each of the Inns of Court functioned as "a propaganda base and general nexus for Puritan clergy and laymen," Gray's Inn was the largest and arguably the most influential.[7]

Though Cambridge was becoming more contentious as the Elizabethan theological consensus disintegrated, Sibbes' change from Cambridge to London gave him a wider view of "the miseries of the times."[8] A number of church issues received public attention: James' perilous allowance of divine-right defenses of episcopacy; the issuance on May 24, 1618, of the *Book of Sport*;[9] and the meeting of the Synod of Dort.

---

5   Reginald J. Fletcher, ed., *The Pension Book of Gray's Inn . . . 1569–1669* (London: 1901), 22, 139; *q.*, 224.

6   *Pension Book*, 224. Joseph Foster, *The Register of Admissions to Gray's Inn, 1521–1889* (London: 1889), 146.

7   Wilfrid Prest, *Inns of Court under Elizabeth I and the Early Stuarts* (London: Rowman and Littlefield, 1972), 38, 207.

8   "Soul's Conflict," in *Works*, 1:244

9   Reprinted in J.R. Tanner, *Constitutional Documents of the Reign of James I, 1603–1625* (Cambridge, England: Cambridge University Press, 1961), 54–56.

In December 1620, James warned the London clergy not to involve themselves in matters of state (as he would do again the following July), and Sibbes knew that this was specially intended to forbid meddling with the betrothal of his son, Charles, to the Catholic Princess Maria Anna of Spain, an arrangement referred to as the Spanish Match. During the preceding month, Sibbes had seen his friend William Gouge imprisoned for treason by James for forwarding the publication of Sir Henry Finch's *The Calling of the Jewes*; after being examined, Gouge was approved and released—but only after nine weeks in prison. Sibbes, living in the shadow of the court, knew something of James' tenderness to criticism, so, while he was not troubled by the church courts, he was not unconcerned with them either. Meanwhile, Sibbes seemed to prosper well enough during this period: his salary was increased twice, and the chapel at Gray's Inn enlarged to accommodate his many hearers.[10]

By 1622, James had begun the sporadic enforcement of a ban on most pulpit discussions of predestination, which would continue in one form or another throughout the rest of Sibbes' life. On August 4, 1622, James sent his "Directions to the Clergy" to George Abbot, archbishop of Canterbury, limiting Sunday afternoon lectures and prohibiting preaching (by any other than bishops or deans) on "the deep points of predestination, election, reprobation or of the universality,

---

10 *Pension Book*, 229, 234, 300; Francis Cowper, *A Prospect of Gray's Inn*, 2nd ed. (London: 1985), 60; Prest, 188.

efficacity, resistibility or irresistibility of God's grace."[11] More ominously for the godly, paragraph five coupled the Puritan with the papist as an "adversary" of the Church of England. (James, fond of referring to the two together, was usually careful to refer only to those who disputed his authority.) Godfrey Davies overstated the effectiveness of this royal order in claiming that this caused "the loss of half the preaching in England."[12] Lectures seem to have continued, though with more caution as to the topics treated.

The following year, James attempted to initiate similar controls through the prohibitions to the press; on September 25, 1623, he issued a proclamation forbidding the printing or importation of books dealing with religion or matters of state until they had been approved.[13] That same year, Sibbes told his hearers at Gray's Inn, "Many there are who think it not only a vain but a dangerous thing to serve God; . . . they count . . . that course which God takes in bringing men to heaven by a plain publishing of heavenly truths, to be nothing but foolishness."[14] In this period of growing concern over public communications, Sibbes uttered what was to become his most controversial statement, in which he enjoined subjection to authority in doubtful matters.[15] Yet, as the negotiations for the

---

11 Reprinted in H. Gee and W.J. Hardy, *Documents Illustrative of English Church History* (London: 1896), 516–18; also, Tanner, 80–82.

12 Davies, 74. Cf. Seaver, 241–42.

13 Tanner, 143–45.

14 "Soul's Conflict," in *Works*, 1:178–79.

15 "Soul's Conflict," in *Works*, 1:209–10.

Spanish Match were at their height, Sibbes said in that same sermon, "Whilst he [Solomon] laboured to find that which he sought for in them, he had like to have lost himself; and seeking too much to strengthen himself by foreign combination, he weakened himself, the more thereby."[16] So, while it may not have been "the calling of those that are subjects, to inquire over curiously into the mysteries of government,"[17] that did not prohibit Sibbes from making pointed comments. As time wore on, the need for such comments increased.

Whatever success James may have enjoyed in creating an inclusive church, Charles I seemed to spurn. Sibbes and his contemporaries could hardly be expected to anticipate the significance for the church in the change of monarchs; to perceive Charles as in any way fundamentally antipathetic to the true Protestant religion would be tantamount to doubting God's providence for the church in England. However, there was no denying that, in Charles, a policy of comprehension had been replaced by one of compression.[18]

In 1624, controversy erupted over a pamphlet by Richard Montagu called "A New Gagg for an Old Goose," in which he stressed the Catholic elements in the Anglican Church and argued that the church was not Calvinist. Alarmed, some Parliamentarians complained to James that the pamphlet

---

16 "Soul's Conflict," in *Works*, 1:219–20. Cf. "The Returning Backslider," in *Works*, 2:252 (probably preached in late 1624).

17 "Soul's Conflict," in *Works*, 1:219–20.

18 Cliffe, 146; cf. Kenneth Fincham, *Prelate as Pastor: The Episcopate of James I* (Oxford, England: Clarendon, 1990), 303.

smacked of Arminianism. Sibbes does not appear to have engaged publicly in this controversy, he was certainly concerned with the growth of "formalism," or lifeless ritualism. In his sermon "The Church's Complaint and Confidence," Sibbes suggests one reason for the plague of 1625: "There is an hypocrisy among men, among a company of formalists, that are the bane of the times, that God will spue out. They are as ill as a profane person in his nostrils."[19] In early 1626, it was clear that something more needed to be done to ensure godly preaching for the people—especially as the nature of the English church itself seemed at stake.[20] William Laud, in his sermon to the new Parliament, openly attacked Calvinism, and the godly were discouraged when James vindicated Montagu.

James died in March 1625 and was succeeded by Charles, but the controversy continued. To quell the debates about Montagu and his writings, Charles dissolved Parliament; the following day, June 16, he issued a "Proclamation for the establishing of the peace and quiet of the Church of England." In this, Charles prohibited controversial or novel preaching that would "in the least degree attempt to violate this bond of peace." Though apparently aimed at the Arminians, the

---

19 Sibbes, "The Church's Complaint and Confidence," in *Works*, 6:196. Cf. "The Sword of the Wicked," in *Works*, 1:114; "Bowels Opened," in *Works*, 2:41, 50; "Excellency," in *Works*, 4:211; "Divine Meditations," in *Works*, 7:228; "The Knot of Prayer Loosed," in *Works*, 7:234, 244, 246.

20 The first recorded meeting of Sibbes and the other Feoffees was four days after the first meeting of the York House Conference.

proclamation had the effect of "stopping the Puritans Mouths, and an uncontrouled Liberty to the Arminian Party."[21]

By 1623, in the shadow of the outbreak of the Thirty Years' War on the Continent, Sibbes had referred to "these times of Jacob's trouble and Zion's sorrow."[22] Concerned about the fortune of his Protestant coreligionists, Sibbes eventually circulated a letter with Gouge, Thomas Taylor, and John Davenport, dated March 2, 1627, appealing for aid for the destitute ministers from the Electorate of the Palatinate in the Holy Roman Empire.[23] For their efforts, Sibbes and his co-petitioners were brought before Laud and the High Commission. While giving aid to the Protestants on the Continent was not inconsistent with English foreign policy, this action could have been seen as an inappropriately direct involvement of private persons in state affairs and therefore as implicit criticism of government inactivity. Furthermore, the court considered the whole question of the Protestant cause on the Continent politically dangerous. A presentation of the events

---

21 Reprinted in Kenyon, *The Stuart Consitution*, 138–39. Cf. John Rushworth, *Historical Collections* (London: 1721), 1:265, 413. Daniel Neal (*The History of the Puritans* [London: 1837], 1:507) mistakenly dated this proclamation as being issued on January 24. This is given further weight by Charles' decision to silence the Oxford Calvinists' attacks on Arminians at the conference at Woodstock on August 23, 1631, called as the result of attacks in sermons at Magdalen Hall and Exeter College. Charles stopped these attacks decisively by dismissing the three preachers from the university, leaving Laud free to reform Oxford. For Laud's accounts of this, see *The Works of the Most Reverend Father in God, William Laud, D.D.* (Oxford, England: 1853), V.i.47–73.

22 "Soul's Conflict," in *Works*, 1:261.

23 Public Records Office, SP16/56, items 15 and 16. Summarized in *Calendar of State Papers, Domestic 1627–1628*, ed. John Bruce (London: 1858), 77.

on the Continent as essentially a Protestant/Roman Catholic war was dangerous to James, because it would severely limit his diplomatic freedom. Therefore, it was in his interest to discourage representations of the war as a war of religion, yet to the godly that is exactly what it was.

Equally important as the plight of their coreligionists on the Continent, however, was that of the godly in England: as "formalism" in the church at home increased and the clergy's ability to comment critically declined, comment upon the situation abroad grew in importance and as such became indirect criticism of trends in the English church.[24] Surely, to both court and clergy, the Continental war was an ongoing illustration of ecclesiastical concerns dominating secular ones and was therefore of apocalyptic interest to both.

By 1628, the godly had seen numerous disappointments. Abroad, the Protestant forces on the Continent seemed near complete collapse, having received a number of serious defeats, and an expedition to relieve the Protestants of La Rochelle had failed. Fearing popular reaction, Charles had forbidden London preachers to take note of it in their sermons.[25] At home, Sibbes, Gouge, Taylor, and Davenport had been reprimanded for their letter urging help for Protestant refugees on the Continent, while William Laud and Richard Neile had been promoted in the church and had both

---

24 "Saint's Safety," in *Works*, 1:318; cf. "Josiah's Reformation," in *Works*, 6:30–34.

25 Bodleian Tanner MS 72/269 (cited "Arminianism" chapter in Julian Davies, *The Caroline Captivity of the Church: Charles I and the Remoulding of Anglicanism: 1625–1641* [Oxford, England: Clarendon, 1992], n148).

been made privy councillors. Meanwhile, John Preston and Richard Stock, both leading godly ministers of London (and old friends of Sibbes) had died, and the publication of John Cosin's popish *A Collection of Private Devotions*—and the collection of forced loans—had provided fresh worries for the godly divines and lawyers. Parliament was incensed; they were even more incensed by Roger Manwaring's preaching, with Charles' approval, that those who opposed the forced loan would burn in hell. As a result, Charles adjourned Parliament, paid Manwaring's fines, formally pardoned him, and gave him the living of Stanford Rivers, Essex. To the godly, these events suggested that the triumph of Roman Catholicism abroad was imminent at home as well.

In November 1628, Charles issued a declaration similar to the Proclamation of 1626, commanding it to be prefixed to all copies of the Articles of Religion,[26] which forbade anyone "to print, or preach, to draw the Article [any of the Thirty-Nine] aside any way, but shall submit to it in the plain and full meaning thereof: and shall not put his own sense or comment to be the meaning of the Article, but shall take it in the literal and grammatical sense."[27] While claiming to promote peace within the church, it served only to confirm the fears of the godly.

---

26 Neal, 1:519–20. Gardiner, *Constitutional Documents*, 75–76; Gee and Hardy, 518–20. Edward Cardwell (*Documentary Annals of the Reformed Church of England* [Oxford, England: 1844], 221–25) for some reason dates the declaration to 1627 (though the notes give 1628).

27 Gardiner, *Constitutional Documents*, 76.

Lectures proliferated throughout early Stuart England, particularly in London; Sibbes may have been right in observing about London "I think there is no place in the world where there is so much preaching."[28] With a population in the hundreds of thousands and clergy who believed that "preaching is that whereby God dispenseth salvation and grace ordinarily,"[29] this is hardly surprising. These lecturers created a situation in which much of the preaching in the city took place outside of normal ecclesiastical lines of authority; Charles and Laud, therefore, seemed to distrust the class of lecturers in general. As bishop of London, Laud persuaded Charles to enact certain restrictions on lecturers, calling them "the Peoples Creatures."[30]

In December 1629, Charles issued his "Instructions," which came close to forbidding preaching without cure of souls.[31] In these instructions, the bishops were enjoined to

---

28 "Lydia's Conversion," in *Works*, 6:527.

29 "Fountain Opened," in *Works*, 5:507.

30 Rushworth (1706), 2:8. Kenyon wrongly represented these restrictions as forbidding corporations to have lecturers (Kenyon, *The Stuarts* [Glasgow, Scotland: 1958], 75), probably based on mistaking Laud's "Considerations" (reprinted in Prynne and summarized in Rushworth)—which had formed the basis of Charles' "Instructions"—for the "Instructions" themselves. Paragraph 5 article 4 of the Instructions merely required a willingness to take up a cure of souls as soon as it may be offered to the lecturer, whereas Laud's "Considerations" had suggested that no lecturer "be suffered to preach till he take upon him Curam Animarum within that Corporation" (Rushworth, 2:8). Seaver noted that this lessening of the requirement was a royal alteration in Laud's more stringent request (Seaver, 244).

31 Laud, vol. V, pt. ii, 307–9; Kenyon, *Stuarts*, 75; Rushworth, 2:8–9; cf. Seaver, 243–44; Prynne, *Canterburies Doome*, 368–73; G.E. Gorman, "A London Attempt to 'tune the pulpit'. Peter Heylyn and his sermon against the Feofees for the purchase of imporpriations," *Journal of Religious History*, vol. VIII/9 (1975): 336; Trevor-Roper, 104–8.

encourage parishes to turn afternoon sermons into catechizing, "that every lecturer do read divine service according to the liturgy printed by authority, in his surplice and hood, before the lecture"; that properly attired, local lecturers be used in market towns; and that "if a corporation maintain a single lecturer, he be not suffered to preach, till he profess his willingness to take upon him a living with cure of souls within that corporation; and that he actually take such benefice or cure, as soon as it shall be fairly procured for him." As a result, Sibbes' friend and fellow in the Feoffees, Thomas Foxley, was deprived of his lectureship, along with others.[32]

During these early years of Charles' reign, Sibbes was very active, launching the Feoffees scheme, cooperating in the letter requesting aid for Protestant refugees, and reforming Katharine Hall as master. His preaching, though not overtly controversial, contained timely remarks. Of the growing irenicism toward Roman Catholicism, Sibbes lamented, "We see nothing in religion, but are as ready to entertain popery as true religion. Is this the fruit of the long preaching of the gospel, and the veil being taken off so long? . . . We are under the seal of God's judgment."[33] Of those who opposed godly preaching, Sibbes said, "It is an argument that a man is in bondage to Satan when he is an enemy any way of the unfolding of the word of God."[34] Thus Sibbes, through his preaching, and

---

32 Prynne, *Canterburies Doome*, 273.
33 "Excellency," in *Works*, 4:304; cf. "The Rich Pearl," in *Works*, 7:260.
34 "Excellency," in *Works*, 4:228.

through other measures, sought to advance the concerns of the godly.

If the newer presentation of Sibbes is one of pacific moderate mystic, the older was one of a battling proto-Dissenter, locked in ecclesiastical combat with Laud. Though this view is a distortion of Sibbes' career, one conflict that did involve Sibbes and Laud surrounded the Feoffees for Impropriations.

In 1625, a group of twelve Londoners "formed themselves into an unincorporated, self-perpetuating group of trustees" in order to "raise funds with which to acquire ecclesiastical revenue in the hands of laymen to be used for the maintenance and relief of a godly, faithful, and painstaking ministry."[35] As they gained control of livings, these Feoffees did not simply fill vacancies with any duly ordained cleric; they replaced holders of benefices with preachers who were of a more radical nature than their predecessors.[36] In his diary, Laud noted under the heading, "Things which I have projected to do if God Bless me in them," as the third of his projects simply "to overthrow the Feoffment, dangerous both to Church and State, going under the specious pretense of buying in Impropriation."[37] Next to this, Laud recorded the single word "Done." In February 1633, after lengthy hearings,[38] the Feoffees were dissolved in

---

35 Isabel M. Calder, *Activities of the Puritan Faction of the Church of England 1625–1633* (London: SPCK, 1957), vii.

36 See Calder, *Activities*, 54–59.

37 William Laud, *History of Troubles* (London: 1695), 68.

38 Arthur Searle, ed., *Barrington Family Letters 1628–1632* (London: 1983), 244.

the Court of Exchequer for having formed a self-perpetuating corporation without having obtained a royal charter.

These conflicts—over the Palatinate letter and the Feoffees—suggest that Sibbes, while judiciously observing his obligations to the church, was not beyond trying the boundaries of those obligations, or at least working apart from them. Such willingness to work within the church did not, however, mark a number of Sibbes' younger friends: soon after the dissolution of the Feoffees, John Cotton was confirmed in his separation from the Church of England, and Thomas Goodwin and John Davenport were soon convinced of the necessity of leaving their livings.

MASTERSHIP OF KATHARINE HALL

It may have been his practice of not "provoking Persons in Power"[39] that led to Sibbes' appointments to the mastership of Katharine Hall in 1626 and to the vicarage of Holy Trinity, Cambridge, in 1633, when other more vocal opponents of Laud were being pushed out.[40] More immediately, it was

---

39 Edmund Calamy, *An Account of the Ministers, Lecturers, Masters and Fellows of Colleges and Schoolmasters, who were Ejected or Silenced after the Restoration in 1660*, 2nd ed. (London: 1713), 2:605–6.

40 Ussher wrote to Archbishop Abbot in January 1627, suggesting that he encourage Sibbes to take the position of Provost at Trinity College, Dublin, because, "I dare undertake that he shall be as observant of you, and as careful to put in execution all your directions, as any man whosoever." Ussher to Abbot, 10 January 1626[7]; found in *The Whole Works of the Most Rev. James Ussher, D.D.*, C.R. Elrington, ed. (Dublin, Ireland: 1864), 16:361.

by the work of Goodwin that Sibbes had become master of Katharine Hall in late 1626.[41] It was not a strange choice; Sibbes had been a senior fellow of St. John's College, one of the largest colleges in the university.

Sibbes was a successful master, bringing in students and benefactions. As a result, his godly influence was felt in the college's religious life, at a time when other colleges were experiencing influence of a decidedly different cast.

Even as master of Katharine Hall,[42] Sibbes exercised his own peculiar brand of moderate reform. One of the more confusing aspects of the small college at this time is the fact that two people named John Ellis were admitted in 1630–31. The older was a Welshman who had taken his B.A. from St. John's, admitted as a fellow in December 1631. The younger John Ellis was a Yorkshireman who matriculated as a student to Katharine Hall in 1630. When a fellowship at Katharine Hall came vacant, Laud had recommended John Ellis, whom Edmund Calamy identified as Laud's "bell-ringer."[43] "Meek persons will bow when others break; they are raised when

---

41 Goodwin, "Memoir . . . out of his own papers," *Works of Thomas Goodwin* (Edinburgh, Scotland: 1861), 2:lxvi. Irvonwy Morgan suggested that this position was obtained for Sibbes by Preston's influence with Buckingham. This is unlikely, because Preston would have had little influence with Buckingham by the winter of 1626 (see Morgan, *Prince Charles's Puritan Chaplain*, 42).

42 For having only six fellows, Katherine Hall boasted an amazing number while Sibbes was there who later became noted persons, including Thomas Goodwin, Andrew Peme, John Arrowsmith, William Strong, Samuel Lynford, John Bond, and William Spurstow.

43 Ellis recounted his debt to Laud in his *S. Austin Imitated: or Retractations and Repentings In reference unto the late Civil and Ecclesiastical Changes in this Nation* (London: 1662), 112.

others are plucked down; . . . these prevail by yielding, and are lords of themselves, and other things else, more than other unquiet-spirited men: the blessings of heaven and earth attend on these."[44] In 1634, Sibbes prevailed by yielding and bowing. The election of the younger John Ellis, the last fellowship election in which Sibbes was to participate, provides a last look at Sibbes' ability to conform. Calamy wrote:

> This was a mighty thing at that time, and intended to be a push upon that Society, with a design either to quarrel with them if they refus'd, or to put a Spy upon them if they accepted. The Doctor [Sibbes], who was not for provoking Persons in Power, told the Fellows, that Lambeth House would be obey'd; that the Person was young, and might prove hopeful, etc. The Fellows yielded.[45]

John Ellis was elected a fellow of the college in December 1634, turning out to be more pliable than moderate, going through Presbyterian and Independent stages and finally conforming at the Restoration. John Knowles, another fellow of the college at that time whom Sibbes had persuaded to vote for Ellis—later one of the ejected Nonconformists of 1662—said, "Fifty Years after, . . . nothing troubled him more, than

---

44 "Soul's Conflict," in *Works*, 1:280. Cf. "Saint's Safety," in *Works*, 1:301.

45 Calamy, 2:605–6. Cf. Benjamin Brook, *The Lives of the Puritans* (London: 1813), 2:419, where the vacancy is mistakenly reported as having occurred in "Magdalen College."

his giving his Vote in that Election."[46] Sibbes' moderation did not always endear him to his contemporaries.

THE SUBSTANCE OF MODERATION

Most of the divisions in the last two decades of Sibbes' life were over the underlying issue of what a true church was, but these divisions shifted according to the perceived needs for, and possibilities of, continuing reform in accord with one's vision of the true church. Thus, to categorize particular ministers according to whether they favored further reform or the status quo can cause the illusion of equivalence between Sibbes and others who otherwise differed greatly. In fact, the substance of Sibbes' defense of the church—godly preaching, right administration of the sacraments, discipline—has more theologically in common with many of those attacking the Elizabethan settlement of his boyhood than with many of his contemporaries' defenses of the establishment of the 1630s. Nevertheless, though Sibbes questioned certain ceremonies, he clearly advocated remaining within the Church of England. By the end of his life, he recognized more clearly than ever that "all Christians in this life have both a different light and a different sight."[47]

There were those, however, who were clearly beyond the pale. As J. Sears McGee has observed, in Sibbes' sermons,

---

46 Calamy, 2:606.
47 "Bride's Longing," in *Works*, 6:549, preached in February, 1634.

any "apparent moderation on the subject of Rome is seen to be ephemeral."[48] Papists came unworthily to the sacraments, and were handicapped in the quest for holiness by their ignorance.[49] His sermons were full of attacks on ceremonialism and formalism, aimed at those within the Church of England, but also those in the Roman church. Arminianism, too, was clearly not to be comprehended in Sibbes' understanding of moderation. In citing and disposing of some of Robert Bellarmine's free will objections, Sibbes was also dealing with the Arminians, in a more politically acceptable way.[50] Although Sibbes' sermons were filled with positive references to Luther,[51] his followers proved a more uncertain object of praise. While rarely critical of Lutherans in his sermons, Sibbes in conversation at one point criticized Philip Melanchthon for his "errors which hee had about Praedestination, as Luther about the Sacrament."[52]

---

48 McGee, *The Godly Man in Stuart England: Anglicans, Puritans, and the Two Tables, 1620–1670* (New Haven, Conn.: 1976), 6. In 1610, Sibbes had been chosen as the B.D. candidate to "respond" at the commencement exercises. He was first to respond to the statement *Romana Ecclesia est apostatica* (BL Harl. MS. 7038, f. 88).

49 Sibbes, "The Right Receiving," in *Works*, 4:65, 68, 73; cf. "Soul's Conflict," in *Works*, 1:138. This piece is an interesting example of Sibbes' understanding of the university as a defense against Rome, charged with protecting the "good deposit of faith."

50 "Bowels Opened," in *Works*, 2:63; "Church's Riches," in *Works*, 4:500; cf. "Excellency," in *Works*, 4:271–72.

51 "Returning Backslider," in *Works*, 2:337; *A Learned Commentary or Exposition Upon The first Chapter of the Second Epistle of S. Paul to the Corinthians* in Works, 3:159, 303, 417; "Excellency," in *Works*, 4:302; "Violence Victorious," in *Works*, 6:311.

52 Hartlib, *Ephemerides*, 1634. Cf. criticism of the Lutherans as idolaters in *A Learned Commentary or Exposition Upon The first Chapter of the Second Epistle of S. Paul to the Corinthians* in *Works*, 3:134, because of their doctrine of consubstantiation.

Sibbes did, of course, favor moderation: "Where most holiness is, there is most moderation, where it may be without prejudice of piety to God and the good of others."[53] He even went so far as to present moderation as the heart of Christianity: "What is the gospel itself but a merciful moderation, in which Christ's obedience is esteemed ours, and our sins laid upon him, and wherein God of a judge becometh the father, pardoning our sins and accepting our obedience, though feeble and blemished!"[54]

Throughout his lifetime Sibbes saw men he respected resign their livings out of scruples about Conformity, but during the last years of his life the church seemed to be hemorrhaging. The occasional Conformists were less tolerated, and men began more openly to choose ministry outside the Church of England. But in this especially, moderation was important in Sibbes' response to those who would separate; such men forgot that "the church of Christ is a common hospital, wherein all are in some measure sick of some spiritual disease or other; that we should all have ground of exercising mutually the spirit of wisdom and meekness."[55] Instead, "for private aims" they wounded the church.[56] Yet years earlier, Sibbes had reminded his hearers of the necessity of coming out of popery and lamented that "it shews the coldness of the times when there is not heat enough of zeal to separate from

---

53 "Bruised Reed," in *Works*, 1:57.

54 "Bruised Reed," in *Works*, 1:58.

55 "Bruised Reed," in *Works*, 1:57

56 "Bruised Reed," in *Works*, 1:76. Cf. *Letters of Davenport*, 39.

a contrary faith."[57] While this was meant to call men out of a growing ceremonialism in the church (or even Rome), it could easily be taken as a pro-Separatist statement. Here Sibbes demonstrated the double-edged nature of the arguments used against Rome.[58] Moderation was clearly in the eye of the beholder: if Rome could be declared apostate, why not the increasingly corrupted Church of England?

This is precisely the question that Sibbes tried to answer in his brief *Consolatory Letter to an Afflicted Conscience*, countering the argument he had used against the Roman church: "But you will say England is not a true Church, and therefore you separate; adhere to the true Church."[59] Sibbes' proof of the Church of England as a true church was that it had all the necessary marks of a true Church—"sound preaching of the Gospell, right dispensation of the Sacraments, Prayer religiously performed, evill persons justly punisht (though not in that measure as some criminals and malefactors deserve)"[60]— and the production of "many spirituall children to the Lord."[61]

---

57 "Soul's Conflict," in *Works*, 1:270.

58 Sibbes clearly was aware of this problem; e.g., "An Exposition of the Third Chapter of the Epistle of St. Paul to the Philippians," in *Works*, 5:68.

59 "Third Chapter Philippians," in *Works*, 5:68.

60 "Consolatory Letter," in *Works*, 1:lxxv.

61 This last was a traditional argument used against the separatists by Sibbes ("Church's Visitation" in *Works*, 1:375–76) as well as Thomas Cartwright decades earlier (cited in Peter Lake, *Moderate Puritans and the Elizabethan Church* [Cambridge: 1982], 87); cf. Thomas Cartwright's Letter to his Sister-in-Law to Dissuade her from Brownism" reprinted in *The Presbyterian Review*, vol. VI [Jan. 1885], 101–11; William Perkins, *The Workes of that Famous and Worthy Minister of Christ in the University of Cambridge, Mr. William Perkins* (London: 1618), 3:389.

"Yea, many of the Separation, if ever they were converted, it was here with us." Even if it England's church was corrupted with ceremonies, Sibbes argued, "must we make a rent in the Church for . . . circumstantiall evils? That were a remedy worse than the disease."[62] He then pointed out that all churches have corruptions, even those more free from ceremonies, "yet . . . are more corrupt in Preachers, (which is the maine) as in prophanation of the Lords day, &C."[63] Sibbes concluded by exhorting his readers:

> There will be a miscellany and mixture in the visible Church, as long as the world endures . . .. So it is no better then soule-murder for a man to cast himselfe out of the Church, either for reall or imaginall corruptions. . . . So let me admonish you to returne your selfe from these extravagant courses, and submissively to render your selfe to the sacred communion of this truly Evangelicall Church of England.[64]

Sibbes' defense of the "truly Evangelicall Church of England" was a brief, powerful one, worked out in his own conscience over many years. No wonder Sibbes gained the reputation for ability to "bring them [Nonconformists] about,

---

62 "Consolatory Letter," in *Works*, 1:lxxv.

63 "Consolatory Letter," in *Works*, 1:lxxvi.

64 "Consolatory Letter," in *Works*, 1:lxxvi.

the best of any about the City of London."[65] As he said, "Sympathy hath a strange force."[66] For all the sympathy Sibbes must have felt for Nonconformists, his attitude about those who would separate from the Church of England was slightly different: the former were obeying their conscience; the latter, usurping roles which God had not given them:

> There is therefore in these judging times good ground of St. James's caveat, that there should not "be too many masters," James iii.l; that we should not smite one another by hasty censures, especially in things of an indifferent nature; some things are as the mind of him is that doth them, or doth them not; for both may be unto the Lord.[67]

Though Separation did not hinder Cotton, Goodwin, and others from remembering Sibbes very positively, there remains no other evidence of how Sibbes came to terms with his friends' leaving the English church.

---

65 John Hacket, *Scrinia Reserata: A Memorial Offer'd to the Great Deservings of John Williams, D.D.* (London: 1693), part i, paragraph 106, pp. 95–96. Cf. John Dury's experience, recounted in John Dury, *The Unchanged, Constant and Single-hearted Peacemaker* (London: 1650), 7.

66 "Soul's Conflict," in *Works*, 1:193.

67 "Bruised Reed," in *Works*, 1:56.

THE DISAPPEARING MIDDLE

Sibbes lived through changes that altered the shape of the
Anglican Church in the early 1600s. He becomes more difficult to understand as he transitioned to his later life, as the
categories that explain him in Cambridge in the 1590s shift
to others appropriate for the 1630s. Presenting Sibbes as a
Nonconformist can be done only with hindsight that sees
every Puritan as a Dissenter and any who voiced objections
as a Nonconformist. Sibbes worked for reform, most actively
around the beginning of Charles' reign; soon though, the
opportunity for action to promote the agendas of preaching
and Protestantism declined. Throughout Sibbes' final years, he
may have felt a growing discouragement, being frustrated by
the shrinking possibility that the church could include those
who would be "reformers without being revolutionaries."[68]

Where did Sibbes' moderation leave his ecclesiology amid
the shifting sands of Stuart Conformity? Time often teases out
inherent contradictions and incipient discord; perhaps this is
what has caused the disparate pictures of Sibbes. He has been
presented as completely neglecting ecclesiology[69]—but on
the other hand, even among those who have more carefully
read his sermons, it seems that Sibbes adopted the rhetoric
of an establishment revolutionary; that is, one who affirmed

---

68 Brian Burch, "The Parish of St. Anne's Blackfriars, London, to 1665," *Guildhall
    Miscellany*, vol. III/1 (October 1969), 30.
69 R.T. Kendall, *Calvin and English Calvinism to 1649* (Oxford, England: 1979), 103.

the established ecclesiology of the Elizabethan church, yet who increasingly emphasized the more voluntary nature of Continental Reformed ecclesiology. As opposition to what Sibbes understood as the preaching of the gospel increased, he became more explicit about the voluntary aspects of the church.[70] Godly preaching, as the means of the Spirit's activity, rather than historical organizational continuity, was the heart of Sibbes' vision of the church.

Victor Morgan wrote of the "latent congregationalism inherent in Puritanism," yet Sibbes did not assert the voluntary nature of the church to the extent of separation, as some did.[71] Why not? Perhaps Sibbes' years provided either a confidence in or a resignation to the establishment, or both, which younger followers could not as easily have had.[72] For

---

70 "Breathing," in *Works*, 2:226. William Bartlet in his *Model of the Primitive Congregational Way* (London, l647), 44–45, realized the way this voluntaristic section of Sibbes could be taken, and used this to support the thesis that one [Sibbes], who was "little thought by most men to have been of this judgement," was in fact a Congregationalist. Collinson (in his "'Magazine,'" *Godly People* [London: 1983], 516) has mistakenly suggested that Simeon Ashe and John Wall later claimed that Sibbes [along with Preston, Dod, and Hildersham] were "zealously affected towards the Presbyterial Government of the Church." Yet, the passage quoted from Wall and Ashe (from their December 1649 preface to Samuel Clarke's, *The Marrow of Ecclesiastical Histories* [London: 1650]) says only that "the latter of these" were so affected—"these" being a long list of sixteen divines, the last eight of whom were nonconformists. Sibbes appears second in the full list. Sibbes had earlier been described as a "Presbyterian" by George B. Dyer in his *History of the University and Colleges of Cambridge* (London: 1814), 2:170.

71 Morgan, "Country, Court and Cambridge University, 1558–1640: A Study in the Evolution of a Political Culture" (Ph.D. diss., University of East Anglia: 1983), 1:59. Note the prevalence of more radical, congregational or independent principles among Sibbes' younger friends.

72 Peter Lake wrote of the essence of moderate Puritanism as the ability to avoid a clash of allegiances between Protestant principle and the national church (Lake,

whatever reason, Sibbes held these two aspects together by taking the establishment to be indifferent, useful insofar as it served the Reformation. In other words, his ecclesiology was subordinated to soteriology in a way Roman Catholics and later Dissenters found impossible to imitate. Yet the changes to the church under the Stuarts shifted the issues around: ecclesiology became more central as it interfered with what strongly Protestant clergy and laity took to be the truly central issue of soteriology. As the issues shifted, Sibbes' position as an establishment revolutionary became more precarious and even compromised. Both sides found him useful as a counter-example to ameliorate stringent remarks about the other side.

If any time could have driven him to open Nonconformity and even separation, it would have been the last two years of his life—yet even they did not. By 1632, Sibbes had seen four preachers at Lincoln's Inn come and go, and three at the Middle Temple. By 1633, only six of the Cambridge heads were more senior than himself, and by 1635, only four. The moderation Sibbes advocated was disappearing. Polarization in the church was increasingly displacing toleration. Yet Sibbes remained a reforming Conformist to the end, even if after 1633 there were few opportunities for such moderate reform beyond his own pulpit. Though he grew more alienated from the power structures of the church—at least in spirit—he was

"Laurence Chaderton and the Cambridge Moderate Puritan Tradition" [Ph.D. diss., University of Cambridge: 1978], 316).

simply too successful and well established, too old, and too tired to be polarized.

As one who had been a child of eleven not far from the coast in 1588, Sibbes would have felt the import of the fate of the Protestants on the Continent more than some; it continued to be a concern until his death. In his final sermon at Gray's Inn, on June 28, 1635, he said, "When there comes ill tidings of the church abroad and at home, it doth not much dismay him. His heart is fixed; he believeth in God and in Christ, and that keeps him from being like a reed shaken with every wind."[73] That evening, Sibbes fell sick. Hartlib noted that, in Sibbes' final days, he was unshaken: "Being asked how hee (Dr. Sips) did in his soule replied I should doe God much wrong if I should not say very well."[74] He was obviously in control of his mental faculties. He finished his preface to *The Soul's Conflict with Itself* the following Wednesday at Gray's Inn. Catlin reported that "his Physitian, that knew his Body best" was "then out of ye Citty."

On Saturday, July 4, Sibbes clearly knew he was dying;[75] that day he revised his will, being "weake in body, but of p'fect memory," leaving his goods to family, friends, and servants at Gray's Inn. For his last six years, Sibbes' home was a rooftop chamber created some years before for Sir Gilbert Gerard, but that had been yielded to Sibbes when Gerard had decided that

---

73 "Two Sermons," in *Works*, 7:355–56.

74 Hartlib, *Ephemerides*, 1635.

75 Sibbes' will, "Grosart Memoir," in *Works*, 1:xxxviii.

he required larger chambers. In this chamber on July 5, 1635 (Commencement Sunday in Cambridge), Sibbes died. He was buried the next day in St. Andrews Holborn, where the members of Gray's Inn had maintained a chapel from medieval times.[76] His funeral sermon, preached by William Gouge, has not survived.

"Our life is nothing but as it were a web woven with interminglings of wants and favours, crosses and blessings, standings and fallings, combat and victory."[77]

---

76 Cowper, 52.
77 "Soul's Conflict," in *Works*, 1:249.

CHAPTER FOUR

Predestination, Covenant, and Conversion

While an investigation of Sibbes as a Reformed theologian could be informative in any case, it is particularly appropriate because he is often presented as having been vague on theological issues, and because Sibbes has been presented as a central figure in the development of moralism, emphasizing sanctification at the expense of justification. This has been argued on the basis of his advocacy of both covenant theology and his understanding of conversion and preparation. Since this second image (as engendering moralism) would fit with the picture of him as lessening a more traditionally Reformed emphasis on divine sovereignty, these issues are best considered together.

PREDESTINATION

The obvious place to begin a study of the Reformed nature of Sibbes' theology is with the doctrine of predestination. As Samuel Brooke, master of Trinity College, Cambridge, told William Laud, the "doctrine of predestination is the root of Puritanism, and Puritanism is the root of all rebellion, and disobedient intractableness in parliament, and all schism and sauciness in the country, nay in the church itself."[1] Yet R.T. Kendall noted "Sibbes' small attention to the doctrine of predestination."[2] While Kendall observed that this may have been due to the restrictions on preaching mentioned in the previous chapter, he wondered, based on "Sibbes' pastoral concern," if Sibbes "would almost prefer that men forget about the decrees of predestination."[3] Small attention, ambiguity, and a desire for his hearers to forget would hardly seem to be the hallmarks of one concerned to present a gospel that was predestined before the foundations of the earth.

---

1   State Papers of Charles I, 16/177/13 (Public Records Office, London); cited by Charles Carlton, *Archbishop William Laud* (London: 1987), 121. Carlton attributed this to Samuel Moore, yet there was no master of Trinity College, Cambridge by this name. It fit, however, Laud's contemporary, Samuel Brooke. Such antipathy is shared by a number of modern historians of the period: e.g., Max Weber, *The Protestant Ethic and the Spirit of Capitalism*, trans. Talcott Parsons (London: Routledge, 1930), 104; William Haller, *The Rise of Puritanism* (New York: Harper, 1938), 83; Pettit, 47; Coward, *The Stuart Age*, 149; Bert Affleck, "The Theology of Richard Sibbes, 1577–1635" (Ph.D. diss., Drew University: 1969), 290.

2   Kendall, *Calvin and English Calvinism to 1649*, 103; cf. Charles H. George, "A Social Interpretation of English Puritanism," *Journal of Modern History*, vol. XXXV/4 (December 1953): 330.

3   Kendall, *Calvin and English Calvinism to 1649*, 103.

Yet while Sibbes' explicit references to predestination may be few, they are neither unclear nor do they seem to have been made reluctantly. Further, any ambiguity or inconsistency on predestination would have been particularly surprising considering the thought he must have given to the matter when he took his bachelor of divinity. The manuscript in the British Library records that he was chosen as the B.D. "respondant" for the 1610 commencement exercises in the university and that the second statement to which he had to respond was "*Dei Decretum non tollit libertatum voluntatis*"—"God's decree will not take away freedoms."[4] Given that the respondent was to answer for two hours, his response could hardly have been slight. Furthermore, in his first introduction of a book to the press eight years later, Sibbes praised Augustine's and Thomas Bradwardine's defenses of predestination.[5] He clearly believed:

First, that there was an eternal separation of men in God's purpose. Secondly, that this first decree of severing man to his ends, is an act of sovereignty over his creature, and altogether independent of anything in the creature, as a cause of it, especially in comparative reprobation, as why he rejected Judas, and not

---

4   BL MS Harl. 7038, f.88.

5   "To the Reader," to Paul Baynes, "A Commentary Upon the First Chapter of the Epistle . . . to the Ephesians," in *Works*, 1:lxxxiv; and again in "First Chapter 2 Corinthians," in *Works*, 3:331. Cf. his criticism of Melanchton for his "errors which hee had about Praedestination," recorded by Hartlib, *Ephemerides*, 1634. Cf. "First Chapter 2 Corinthians," in *Works*, 3:134.

Peter; sin foreseen cannot be the cause, because that was common to both, and therefore could be no cause of severing. Thirdly . . . that damnation is an act of divine justice, which supposeth demerit; and therefore the execution of God's decree is founded on sin, either of nature, or life, or both.[6]

REPROBATION

The debates over the nature and working of predestination were most heated concerning the doctrine of reprobation—the doctrine that, even as God had eternally decreed to save some, so He had also eternally decreed to damn some.[7] If the decrees of election and reprobation were to be maintained in strictest parallel, then both of them must be irrespective of individual merit or demerit, but based on God's sovereignty alone.

When it came to reprobation, Sibbes was not so much silent as quiet on the issue. When he did speak of the reprobate, he did so in one of two ways: sometimes he used the word simply to refer to those who were presently outside of Christ,[8] but he also used the word to refer to the fact that Christ "hath predestinated and elected us, and refused others."[9] Echoing

---

6   "To the Reader," in "First Chapter Ephesians," 1:lxxxv.

7   Clearly stated by William Perkins in *The Workes of that Famous and Worthy Minister of Christ in the University of Cambridge, Mr. William Perkins* (London: 1616), 1:24–25.

8   E.g., "First Chapter 2 Corinthians," in *Works*, 4:323.

9   "Bowels Opened," in *Works*, 2:181; cf. "Salvation Applied," in *Works*, 5:389.

Paul about Pharaoh in Romans 9, Sibbes referred to those who "had rather lose their souls than their wills" as those who "are but raised up for Christ to get himself glory in their confusion."[10] He did not assume that eternal reprobation was the case of any particular individual listening—nor could he—because, as he said repeatedly, this was part of "God's secret purpose" hidden in this world,[11] and their very presence in the hearing of the Word was cause for hope rather than despair.[12] Discouraging his hearers from delving too deeply into this discussion,[13] Sibbes exhorted them simply to trust.[14]

Sibbes seemed to agree that damnation must always come from God's judgment on sin,[15] and thus was concerned that a decree of reprobation presented too starkly would dishonor God. Ultimately, Sibbes insisted that the damned have only themselves to blame for their fate,[16] stating that "there was never any yet came to hell, but they had some seeming pretence for their coming thither."[17]

---

10 "Bruised Reed," in *Works*, 1:93; cf. "Salvation Applied," in *Works*, 5:390; "Saint's Safety," in *Works*, 1:321.

11 "Salvation Applied," in *Works*, 5:390; cf. *A Learned Commentary or Exposition Upon The fourth Chapter of the Second Epistle of Saint Paul to the Corinthians*, in *Works*, 4:377.

12 "Description of Christ" in *Works*, 1:23; cf. "Saint's Hiding-Place," in *Works*, 1:410; "Bruised Reed," in *Works*, 1:48, 72; "Fourth Chapter 2 Corinthians," in *Works*, 4:377.

13 "Salvation Applied," in *Works*, 5:390.

14 "Fountain Opened," in *Works*, 5:511.

15 "Fountain Opened," in *Works*, 5:510–11; "Salvation Applied," in *Works*, 5:389.

16 "Bowels Opened," in *Works*, 2:69; cf. "The Matchless Love and Inbeing" in *Works*, 6:406; "Description," in *Works*, 1:25; "Christ is Best; or, St. Paul's Strait," in *Works*, 1:337–38.

17 "Bowels Opened," in *Works*, 2:87.

PARTICULAR REDEMPTION

The other issue that could create pastoral problems for doubting souls was that of the extent of Christ's atonement. In short: If God elected only some to salvation, then for whom did Christ die?

There is some ambiguity in Sibbes' sermons on this, perhaps because of his desire to be a faithful exegete of Scripture. One finds statements that "He [Christ] was a public person. Upon the cross he stood in the place of all the world, and all their sins committed, or foreseen to be committed, lay upon him."[18] Yet in context, he only intended by this to show that Christ's resurrection foreshadows the resurrection to life of "every true Christian." Consistent with his Reformed theology, Sibbes taught that "when Christ is said to redeem the world, it must not be understood generally of all mankind."[19] Instead, "Christ died alone and singular in this respect; because in him dying all died that were his, whom the Father gave him to die for. They go in parallel, God's gift and Christ's death."[20]

---

18 "The Power of Christ's Resurrection," in *Works*, 5:198.

19 "Fountain Opened," in *Works*, 5:516–17.

20 "Christ's Exaltation," in *Works*, 5:345. Cf. "Salvation Applied," in *Works*, 5:388; "Bowels Opened," in *Works*, 2:179; "Judgment," in *Works*, 4:103; "Christ's Sufferings for Man's Sin," in *Works*, 5:356. Karl Barth, in his criticism of federal or covenant theology, presented the doctrine of a "limited" atonement as being one of the necessary results. Karl Barth, *Church Dogmatics*, trans. G.W. Bromiley (Edinbugh, Scotland: T&T Clark,1956), vol. IV/I, 57. J.B. Torrance follows partway in this assessment, "Covenant or Contract?" *Scottish Journal of Theology*, vol. XXIII/1 (Feb. 1970): 68–69.

When Sibbes referred to "God's secret purpose in electing some, and redeeming some," he was not repeating himself in poetic parallelism but making two distinct points: God has elected only some, and Christ, by His death, has redeemed only some.[21] This was not to introduce a smallness into consideration of the atonement; both the extent and limitation of Christ's atonement were matters of praise.[22]

In his only surviving long discussion of this doctrine, Sibbes reasoned from Romans 5:10 that "the greatest part are not saved by his life, therefore they are not reconciled by his death."[23] He assumed that his opponents on this point would be "papists"[24] who wished to add individual merit into salvation. Yet Sibbes' affirmation of this doctrine is, in most of his sermons, more evident in its assumption than in exposition.[25]

ELECTION

When speaking of predestination, Sibbes usually spoke of election,[26] which is the particular predestination of certain individuals to salvation,[27] and which therefore fit perfectly with Sibbes' desire to speak of Christianity affectionately, as

---

21 "Salvation Applied," in *Works*, 5:390.

22 "Rich Pearl," in *Works*, 7:257; "Salvation Applied," in *Works*, 5:389.

23 "Salvation Applied," in *Works*, 5:388; cf. "Pattern," in *Works*, 7:509.

24 "Salvation Applied," in *Works*, 5:389, 392.

25 E.g., "Angels," in *Works*, 6:354; "Salvation Applied," in *Works*, 5:389–91; "Church's Riches," in *Works*, 4:525.

26 "Lydia," in *Works*, 6:523.

27 "Privileges," in *Works*, 5:262.

the story of God's love. When speaking of the elect, he meant those marvelously, lovingly chosen by God the Father for salvation before time and in time.[28] To be elect meant to be God's.

This "world taken out of the world, the world of the elect"[29] is composed of people specially favored, those whom God calls His "best friends."[30] They are God's before they ever respond to the ministry of the Word.[31] They are not all who professed to be Christians, but those whom the Father had given to the Son before the creation of the world. They are those for whom the Son died, the "true professors of the truth" drawn by the Spirit through the ministry of the Word, moving to perfection "by degrees." They never fall away, but certainly spend eternity together with God.[32] It was only by being in Christ that the believer could have any certainty that he was one of the elect.[33]

Election was, for Sibbes, something not to be debated, but demonstrated.[34] If to be among the elect was to be one to whom God had reconciled Himself, and who had been

---

28 "Description," in *Works*, 1:9; cf. "Bowels Opened," in *Works*, 2:73; "Rich Poverty," in *Works*, 6:241.

29 "Fountain Opened," in *Works*, 5:516; "Judgment's Reason," in *Works*, 4:98.

30 "Breathing," in *Works*, 2:216; cf. "Rich Poverty," in *Works*, 6:232, 235; "Soul's Conflict," in *Works*, 1:262.

31 "Bowels Opened," in *Works*, 2:142; "Of the Providence of God," in *Works*, 5:50–51.

32 "Breathing," in *Works*, 2:234; "Bowels Opened," in *Works*, 2:36, 83, 179; "Demand," in *Works*, 7:482; "Excellency," in *Works*, 4:218; "The Faithful Covenanter," in *Works*, 6:8; "Judgment," in *Works*, 4:103; "The Difficulty of Salvation," in *Works*, 1:396.

33 "Description," in *Works*, 1:9,18; "Soul's Conflict," in *Works*, 1:132.

34 "Church's Riches," in *Works*, 4:520–21; cf. "Bowels Opened," in *Works*, 2:69. Sylvia

reconciled to God, then nothing could be more important for the Christian than seeking and securing evidence of election.[35] Yet such assurance was not to be found by speculations of the "dark scruples of his eternal decree! Obey the command, obey the threatening, and put that out of doubt. If thou yield to the command, if thou obey the threatening, if thou be drawn by that, undoubtedly thou art the child of God."[36] By speaking of election in his sermons, Sibbes meant not to grow pride, but gratitude,[37] not to enervate the elect, but rather to energize them to action.[38]

Though Sibbes largely avoided controversy over predestination and referred to it sparingly, it cannot reasonably be suggested that he had doubts about the doctrine's truth or use. In his sermons, all the doctrines associated with predestination were present: election, reprobation, the decrees, and definite atonement.

Roberts, "'Radical Graces': A Study of Puritan Casuistry in the Writings of William Perkins and Richard Sibbes" (M.A. thesis, University of Melbourne: 1972), 183.

35 "Right Receiving," in *Works*, 4:62–63; "Soul's Conflict," in *Works*, 1:137.

36 "First Chapter 2 Corinthians," in *Works*, 3:156; cf. "Glance of Heaven," in *Works*, 4:182.

37 "First Chapter 2 Corinthians," in *Works*, 3:331; "Rich Poverty," in *Works*, 6:234; "Bowels Opened," in *Works*, 2:142; cf. "Breathing," 2:234; "Bowels Opened," in *Works*, 2:73; "Divine Meditations," in *Works*, 7:216; "Excellency," in *Works*, 4:218; "Faithful Covenanter," in *Works*, 6:8; "Privileges," in *Works*, 5:264; "Soul's Conflict," in *Works*, 1:184, 264; "Fountain Opened," in *Works*, 5:529; "Description," in *Works*, 1:9.

38 "Bowels Opened," in *Works*, 2:36, 83; "Bruised Reed," in *Works*, 1:49; "Demand," in *Works*, 7:478, 482, 491; "Excellency," in *Works*, 4:282; "Soul's Conflict," in *Works*, 1:206–7, 250; "Church's Riches," in *Works*, 4:517; "Fountain Opened," in *Works*, 5:490, 532; "Judgment's Reason," in *Works*, 4:103; "Rich Poverty," in *Works*, 6:235, 241; "Privileges," in *Works*, 5:257; "Providence," in *Works*, 5:50–51.

Yet this did not give to Sibbes' sermons a grimness that some writers present as necessary to any espousal of such doctrines. Instead, Sibbes' discussions of predestination always had a positive purpose and were pastoral and personal. For Sibbes, the Reformed doctrines of predestination were nothing other than God's love language to his people, a "delightful determinism."[39]

It may fairly be asked, though, why Sibbes was reluctant to discuss the doctrine explicitly. Four reasons suggest themselves: first, during his time in London, the pulpit and press knew increasing controls. Second, part of the reason that precipitated official discouragement from preaching on predestination—the doctrine's popularity—suggests why he could have felt so little need to do so, as his clerical circles, and most of his audiences, were composed of those who would have agreed on predestination.

A third reason may be the form of address that Sibbes most extensively used: the sermon. Sibbes' longest discussion of predestination comes in one of the few non-sermonic pieces of his writings: the preface to a book. Sermons were for lay edification, not university disputation. Some very difficult pastoral issues were involved in contemplation of the doctrines of election and predestination.

Finally, there is the matter of his personality. From Jenison's 1621 reference to Sibbes' "timourousness" to his posthumous

---

39 Harold Shelly, "Richard Sibbes: Early Stuart Preacher of Piety (Ph.D. diss., Temple University: 1972), 137.

reputation as being personally humble and noncontroversial, Sibbes gives the impression of a pacific figure. Regardless of the political situation, the pastoral situation always seems to find predestination an unpacific doctrine (whether for good or ill). It would be consistent with what we know to suggest that, given the controversy which so easily arose from it, he considered it a topic better dealt with outside the pulpit.

COVENANT, CONVERSION, AND PREPARATION

Many have suggested that the early seventeenth-century English Protestant preachers and theologians were in the forefront of a sea change in Protestant theology, from monergism—wherein God acts alone to save—to synergism—wherein men cooperate with the grace of God in salvation—through the idea of covenant.[40] Sibbes, it is said, was among those at the forefront of this shift. Was Sibbes a covenant theologian? Was this

---

40 Pettit, 218. It has been suggested that the sheerness of the sixteenth-century Reformers' doctrine of the sovereignty of God was undermined by their successors' use of covenant imagery. The number of books and articles on the modification of Reformed theology by the concept of covenant is vast; some are cited below. E.g., Christopher Hill's statement that "covenant theology, and the suggestion that a hearty desire for salvation might be the first evidence of grace at work in a man's soul, were desperate attempts to make Calvinism palatable for mass consumption" (*Society and Puritanism in Pre-Revolutionary England* [London: 1964], 489); elsewhere, Hill referred to covenant theology as "a means . . . of smuggling 'works' into Calvinism" (*Puritanism and Revolution* [London: Secker and Warburg, 1958], 240); Norman Pettit's statement that "the extreme emphasis on covenant ideals . . . contradicted the dogmatic stand that anything done on man's part diminishes God's sovereignty" (218).

covenantal framework in tension with his orthodox Protestant teaching of predestination and election?

The uses of "covenant" among the godly of Sibbes' time seemed to be two: primarily in description of God's saving covenant, and secondarily in description of the obligations of the Christian to God and others. The first sense intended no synergism, and the second sense included the obligations on both parts as fundamental to the existence of the covenant.[41]

John Knewstub "took the covenant pattern so completely for granted that the word itself appears only now and then, quite casually."[42] For example, throughout his exposition of Exodus 20, Knewstub used much legal language; in preaching on the Ten Commandments, he intended that his hearers understand the obligations under which they stood as God's covenant people. In his epistle dedicatory, he stated that one sermon "will declare with what conditions we have wages promised for our work, and whether the covenant be so favorable as that we need not to doubt but that we shall be able to perform it."[43] Yet Knewstub also used "covenant" interchangeably with the more obviously unilateral

---

41 E.g., "Bride's Longing," in *Works*, 6:542; Hebrews 9:16–17.

42 Leonard Trinterud, *Elizabethan Puritanism* (Oxford, England: Oxford University Press, 1971), 313.

43 Knewstub, *Lectures … upon the Twentieth Chapter of Exodus and Certain Other Places of Scripture* (1577; repr. in Trinterud, Elizabethan Puritanism), 316.

"promise"[44] and denied that the basis of the covenant could ever be bilateral.[45]

Sibbes seems to have assumed the centrality of covenant in a manner that was in keeping with that of his teachers and contemporaries. William Perkins, for instance, spoke of the covenant of grace in a way that showed that it was both essential to be a part of it, yet beyond any one's ability to enter it savingly. In so doing, Perkins sought both to encourage people to rely on God and to grow gratitude in those who thought themselves already in the covenant of grace.[46] In Perkins's sermons, the "covenant-God offered grace and demanded obedience, but he did not recompense obedience by offering grace."[47]

Along these lines, Sibbes and John Davenport, in their introduction to one of the most important statements of early-seventeenth-century English covenant theology, wrote, "We send forth these sermons of God's All-Sufficiency, and Man's Uprightness, and the Covenant of Grace first . . . because the right understanding of these points hath a chief influence into a Christian life."[48] Likewise, in Sibbes' sermons, covenant was central.[49]

---

44 Knewstub, 321; cf. 322–24.

45 Knewstub, 324.

46 William Perkins, *A Clowd of Faithfull Witnesses, Leading to the heavenly Canaan: Or, A Commentarie upon the 11. Chapter to the Hebrewes, preached in Cambridge …* (n.l.: 1609), 2, 27.

47 [Sibbes and John Davenport], "To the Reader," to John Preston, *The New Covenant, or the Saints Portion* (1629); rept. in *Works,* 1:xcvi.

48 [Sibbes and John Davenport], "To the Reader," to John Preston, *The New Covenant, or the Saints Portion* (1629); repr. in *Works,* 1:xcvi.

49 "Miller, "Marrow," 257; Roberts, 108.

COVENANT MEMBERSHIP

The first question concerns who is included in the covenant. Sibbes taught that whoever has been baptized is in the covenant.[50] The covenant is "made in baptism"[51] and "renewed in taking of the Lord's supper."[52] That is not to say that all who are in the covenant are saved; there is an inward baptism and an outward baptism. "The inward, which is the washing of the soul; the outward doth not save without the inward. Therefore he prevents them, lest they should think that all are saved by Christ that are baptized, that have their bodies washed outwardly with water."[53]

Sibbes taught that there are obligations and requirements in the covenant of grace.[54] The primary requirement, as represented in the baptismal service, is trusting[55] or faith.[56] He

---

50 "Lydia," in *Works*, 6:530–31; cf. "Knot of Prayer," 7:249.

51 "Demand," 7:487; cf. 483; "Faithful Covenanter," 6:24.

52 "Demand," 7:490; cf. "Faithful Covenanter," 6:24; "David's Conclusion; or, the Saint's Resolution" in *Works*, 7:90; "Lydia," in *Works*, 6:530–31; "Epistle to the Christian Reader," to Ezekiel Culverwell, *Treatise of Faith* (London: 1623); repr. in *Works*, 1:xc–xciii; "Soul's Conflict," in *Works*, 1:212; "Fountain Opened," in *Works*, 5:462, 469; William Perkins, "The Foundation of Christian Religion Gathered into Six Principles" in *The Work of William Perkins*, ed. Ian Breward (Appleford, Abingdon, Berkshire, England: Sutton Courtenay, 1970),163; Perkins, *Workes*, 1:71–77; William Gouge, *A Learned and Very Useful Commentary on the Whole Epistle to the Hebrews* (London: 1655), pt. viii, 45.

53 "Demand," in *Works*, 7:479; cf. "Excellency," in *Works*, 4:219; "First Chapter 2 Corinthians," in *Works*, 3:462; "Bowels Opened," in *Works*, 2:169. Though "First Chapter 2 Corinthians," in *Works*, 3:451, could be taken as assuming baptismal regeneration, upon careful reading in context, it clearly does not.

54 "Demand," in *Works*, 7:482; cf. "Fountain Opened," in *Works*, 5:511.

55 "Rich Poverty," in *Works*, 6:254; cf. "Yea and Amen," in *Works*, 4:127.

56 "Demand," in *Works*, 7:482.

wrote, "We that will answer to the covenant made in baptism must perform it, especially that that we then covenanted. What was that? We answered that we would believe. Dost thou believe? I believe every article of the faith. And do you renounce the devil and all his works? I do. Therefore, unless now we believe in Christ, and renounce the devil, we renounce our baptism. It doth us no good."[57]

This trust or faith in Christ must be sincere, and Sibbes reminded his hearers that this sincerity was not to lead to inaction. Indeed, believers are to "perform" the covenant of grace.[58] To this end, he exhorted his hearers to "often renew our covenants and purposes every day."[59]

Sibbes clearly taught that there are promises of God that are conditional. For example, in commenting upon 2 Corinthians 1:20, Sibbes divided promises that are "absolute, without any condition" (e.g., the coming of Christ, His return, the final resurrection) from those that are "conditional, in the manner of propounding, but yet absolute in the real performance of them" (e.g., forgiveness of sins if one believes and repents).

Yet even these latter types are absolute, even though they are propounded conditionally. This is because God performs

---

57 "Demand," in *Works*, 7:487; cf. 488–91.

58 "Bride's Longing," in *Works*, 6:541–42; "Rich Poverty," in *Works*, 6:252; "Pattern," in *Works*, 7:514–15. Cf. Gouge, pt. viii, 39.

59 "Angels," in *Works*, 6:345; cf. "Judgment," in *Works*, 4:94; "Faithful Covenanter," in *Works*, 6:24; "Bowels Opened," in *Works*, 2:16; "Church's Visitation," in *Works*, 1:381; "Demand," in *Works*, 7:490–91; "Judgment," in *Works*, 4:111; "Two Sermons," in *Works*, 7:345; "Returning Backslider," in *Works*, 2:269.

the covenant Himself; He performs our part and His own too. For since Christ, though He propounded the promises of the gospel with conditions, yet He performs the condition; He stirs us up to attend upon the means, and by His Spirit in the Word He works faith and repentance, which is the condition. Faith and repentance are His gift.[60]

It is clear that Sibbes frequently used covenant terminology, and that this in no way eclipsed the gratuitous nature of salvation. Sibbes simply said that "in the covenant of grace, God intends the glory of his grace above all."[61] As if knowing some of the interpretations to be put on his sermons later, Sibbes rebuked his hearers, saying, "It is a childish thing from them to infer that there is power in man, becuase God persuadeth and exhorts."[62]

CONVERSION

Perry Miller observed that the doctrine of conversion "holds in miniature almost every characteristic of Puritan thinking."[63] Conversion was what Sibbes exhorted church members to prepare themselves, yet it was also presented as fundamentally

---

60 "First Chapter 2 Corinthians," in *Works*, 3:394; cf. 521; "Bride's Longing," in *Works*, 6:541–42; "Yea and Amen," in *Works*, 4:122.

61 "Divine Meditations," in *Works*, 7:189.

62 "Fourth Chapter 2 Corinthians," in *Works*, 4:385.

63 Miller, *Mind*, 287. Cf. Alan Simpson, *Puritanism in Old and New England* (Chicago: University of Chicago Press, 1955), 2–6.

God's action. How could the monergism implied in Sibbes' theology be blended with human action in conversion?

According to Sibbes, the Spirit does not simply persuade; He enlightens the elect by opening the eyes of the soul to God, because "a carnal eye will never see spiritual things."[64] Sibbes saw conversion as the Spirit's action in enlightenment as transforming the soul.[65] No one will be converted apart from the Spirit's work, for the ability to move to God is itself a radical change in the fallen soul. "It is no matter how dull the scholar be, when Christ taketh upon him to be the teacher."[66] Grace is irresistible.[67] "As the minister speaks to the ear, Christ speaks, opens, and unlocks the heart at the same time; and gives it power to open, not from itself, but from Christ. . . . The manner of working of the reasonable creature, is to work freely by a sweet inclination, not by violence. Therefore when he works the work of conversion, he doth it in a sweet manner, though it be mighty for the efficaciousness of it."[68] In conversion, the

---

64 "Bruised Reed," in *Works*, 1:59; cf. "Soul's Conflict," in *Works*, 1:172, 214, 269.

65 See chapters 31 and 32 of Augustine, "On Grace and Free Will," *Anti-Pelagian Writings*, trans. Peter Holmes (Grand Rapids, Mich.: 1971), beginning on 456; Augustine, *Enchiridion*, trans. Ernest Evans (London: SPCK, 1953), 28–30; Calvin, *Institutes*, 2.4.8; Perkins, *Galatians*, 44; *Works*, 1:79.

66 "Bruised Reed," in *Works*, 1:52; cf. 83, 93–94; "Fountain Opened," 5:468. On conversion in Sibbes, Thomas Hooker, and Thomas Shepherd as alteration of judgment, see Stoever, 61–63.

67 "Bruised Reed," in *Works*, 1:95; cf. "Fourth Chapter 2 Corinthians," in *Works*, 4:385.

68 "Bowels Opened," in *Works*, 2:63; cf. "Fountain Opened," in *Works*, 5:468; "Bruised Reed," in *Works*, 1:81; "Excellency," in *Works*, 4:218, 233–34; "Pattern," in *Works*, 7:511.

Spirit opens the heart,[69] making it fruitful,[70] by presenting true knowledge of God to the soul—"the sight of their misery and the sight of God's love in Christ"[71]—thereby enabling the soul to see that to which it was blind. Only at conversion is the soul liberated; only then does it become truly free. "Those that take the most liberty to sin are the most perfect slaves," Sibbes said,[72] true freedom only comes in freedom toward the good.[73]

Even more radical images for conversion are common in Sibbes' sermons.[74] Conversion "is an alteration, a change, a new man, a new creature, new birth, &c. We see the necessity of a change."[75] Nevertheless, conversion necessarily incorporated actions of both God and man.[76] Men are presented as agents in their own, and others', conversions.[77] Belief is necessary;[78] therefore, Sibbes exhorted his hearers to "get into

---

69 "Bowels Opened," in *Works*, 2:8; cf. "Lydia," in *Works*, 6:521–25.

70 "Bowels Opened," in *Works*, 2:9.

71 "Bowels Opened," in *Works*, 2:160. Cf. John Preston, *The Breast-Plate of Faith and Love* (London: 1634), pt. i, 47–49, 162.

72 "Bruised Reed," in *Works*, 1:97; "Excellency," in *Works*, 4:226–27.

73 See Augustine, *De libero arbitrio*, 2:13; Anselm, "Proslogion," in *A Scholastic Miscellany: Anselm to Ockham*, ed. and trans. E.R. Fairweather (London: Westminster John Knox, 1956), 77; Calvin, *Institutes*, 2.3.5; Perkins, *Galatians*, 46, 318.

74 "Excellency," in *Works*, 4:259.

75 "Excellency," in *Works*, 4:259; cf. 221, 272; "Bowels Opened," in *Works*, 2:24–25.

76 "Bruised Reed," in *Works*, 1:47; cf. "Bowels Opened," in *Works*, 2:24,179; "Rich Poverty," in *Works*, 6:242; Stoever, 8.

77 "Bowels Opened," in *Works*, 2:36, 69, 167; cf. "Judgment," in *Works*, 4:85; "Returning," in *Works*, 2:255; "Fourth Chapter 2 Corinthians," in *Works*, 4:449; "Fountain Opened," in *Works*, 5:513; "Power of Resurrection," in *Works*, 5:199; "Providence," in *Works*, 5:37; Perkins, *Galatians*, 46.

78 "Power of Resurrection," in *Works*, 5:198.

Christ"[79] and the covenant with him,[80] to "run after him" and to "open unto him,"[81] to "trust God . . . now."[82] Yet even this consent, which we must "labour to bring our hearts," is "wrought":[83] although "his subjects are voluntaries," they "seek for heaven in hell that seek for spiritual love in an unchanged heart."[84] At conversion, "we had nothing good in us," when the Spirit came to the soul "it met with nothing but enmity, rebellion, and indisposedness,"[85] "we resisted;"[86] our hearts were "unyielding and untractable."[87] Conversion is an even greater work of God's than creation, because at creation, "he had to do with simply nothing. But when God comes to make the heart believe, he finds opposition and rebellion. He finds man against himself."[88] Christ must therefore wound[89] and give new life.[90] Our rebellious spirits must be "overpowered

---

79 "Bowels Opened," in *Works*, 2:187.

80 "Knot of Prayer," in *Works*, 7:249.

81 "Bowels Opened," in *Works*, 2:10.

82 "Soul's Conflict," in *Works*, 1:202. Cf. Calvin, *Institutes*, 3.2.1. Perkins, too, exhorted people to "labour for a sound and saving faith," *Hebrewes*, 26, 29; cf. 31–32.

83 "Fountain Opened," in *Works*, 5:486. Cf. Calvin, *Institutes*, 3.2.33; Perkins, *Galatians*, 45; *Work*, ed. Breward, 156–57; Preston, *Breast-Plate*, pt. i, 165; Westminster Confession of Faith 10.2; Stoever, 106–9.

84 "Bruised Reed," in *Works*, 1:79–80; cf. "The Christian's End" in *Works*, 5:308; "Pattern," in *Works*, 7:510.

85 "Bowels Opened," in *Works*, 2:48.

86 "Bowels Opened," in *Works*, 2:73; cf. "Bruised Reed," in *Works*, 1:96.

87 "Bruised Reed," in *Works*, 1:44–45.

88 "Fountain Opened," in *Works*, 5:519; cf. "Power of Resurrection," in *Works*, 5:198–99; "Soul's Conflict," in *Works*, 1:152; "Excellency," in *Works*, 4:225, 245; Preston, *Breast-Plate*, pt. i, 165–66.

89 "Bruised Reed," in *Works*, 1:46.

90 "Bruised Reed," in *Works*, 1:95. Cf. "Fountain Opened," in *Works*, 5:495; Calvin,

with grace."[91] Echoing Augustine, Sibbes said, "God knoweth we have nothing of ourselves, therefore in the covenant of grace he requireth no more than he giveth, and giveth what he requireth, and accepteth what he giveth."[92]

PREPARATION

Given that conversion is enabled and made certain by God, what is the role of man and means in this turning? This is the issue that has come to be called "preparationism." Ambiguity is particularly dangerous in this question, because one can lose sight of the point of such preparation. For what is one being prepared? Sibbes spoke of preparation for good works,[93] self-denial,[94] trials,[95] the second coming,[96] reception of the sacrament,[97] hearing the Word,[98] prayer,[99] coming to church,[100] and conver-

---

Institutes, 2.5.14.

91 "Ungodly's Misery," in *Works*, 1:392; cf. "Bowels Opened," in *Works*, 2:10, 106, 182, 187; "Excellency," in *Works*, 4:244; "Soul's Conflict," in *Works*, 1:265.

92 "Bruised Reed," in *Works*, 1:58.

93 "Bruised Reed," in *Works*, 1:75.

94 "Third Chapter Philippians," in *Works*, 5:82; "Rich Pearl," in *Works*, 7:258.

95 "Providence," in *Works*, 5:53; "Soul's Conflict," in *Works*, 1:163, 249.

96 "Bride's Longing," in *Works*, 6:551–52.

97 "First Chapter 2 Corinthians," in *Works*, 3:134, 528; "Angels," in *Works*, 6:336–7; "Bowels Opened," in *Works*, 2:193; "Judgment," in *Works*, 4:88–89; RR.IV.62. This theme is made prominent in Sibbes' sermons due to the fact that so many of his sermons were preached before the Lord's Supper (e.g., "Right Receiving, Judgement's Reason").

98 "Providence," in *Works*, 5:36, 53.

99 "Bowels Opened," in *Works*, 2:17–18; "Knot of Prayer," in *Works*, 7:246.

100 "Fountain Opened," in *Works*, 5:465.

sion.[101] Carelessness has led some to take any statement of or call for human action—found on every page of Sibbes' works —as proof of "preparationism." Some also have confused the issue by taking descriptive passages in sermons as prescriptive ones, misunderstanding sections describing various stages in the Christian's journey as instructions about what they should do next[102] and assuming that adherence to a theology of predestination also necessitates a belief in an immediate conversion, one that is inconsistent with natural human faculties.[103]

Yet this reading of Sibbes is faulty, for two reasons. First, Sibbes' theology of reprobation accounted for those who would never respond savingly to the gospel, termed by Sibbes the "eternal reprobates." Though he thought he would never know who they were, he believed that his preaching only added to their condemnation. However, he also referred more generally to those living wicked lives—who were not at present in Christ—as reprobates, again indiscernable from the others, and assumed their presence in his congregations; it was to these that his exhortations to conversion were addressed. Though he exhorted unbelievers to come to Christ, and assumed that they were obligated by God to do so, this does

---

101 "Bowels Opened," in *Works*, 2:166; "Excellency," in *Works*, 4:296. Perhaps Sibbes' most clear exposition of the "works of preparation" for conversion, is found in Sibbes' sermon "Lydia," in *Works*, 6:522–23.

102 Cf. Lynn Baird Tipson Jr., "The Development of a Puritan Understanding of Conversion" (Ph.D. diss., Yale University: 1972), 322; "Lydia," in *Works*, 6:522.

103 Pettit, 17.

not mean—in keeping with the Augustinian tradition—that he assumed that they had the ability.

Given Sibbes' pastoral situation—preaching almost entirely to congregations full of members of the covenant—it is unsurprising that he should have said that "God usually prepares those that he means to convert, as we plough before we sow."[104] Sibbes spent the bulk of his time exhorting regular hearers to use the means of grace to make certain of their conversion and "stablish" their faith.[105] Yet he was careful to say that "all preparations are from God. We cannot prepare ourselves, or deserve future things by our preparations; for the preparations themselves are of God."[106] Lest anyone think that any action, however required or useful, could be a source of pride, Sibbes preached that "it is a sottish conceit to think that we can fit ourselves for grace, as if a child in the womb could forward its natural birth. If God hath made us men, let us not make ourselves gods."[107]

Sibbes taught that the primary means Christ used to

---

104 "Lydia," in *Works*, 6:522. Calvin, too, was such a "preparationist"; see, for example, *Deuteronomie*, 423, where he asserted that God "prepareth our hearts to come unto him and to receive his doctrine," clearly referring to conversion.

105 "Pattern," in *Works*, 7:510–11; "The Fruitful Labour for Eternal Food," in *Works*, 6:380.

106 "Lydia," in *Works*, 6:522; cf. "Josiah," in *Works*, 6:33; "Bruised Reed," in *Works*, 1:51, 72, 74; "Returning Backslider," in *Works*, 2:404; "Excellency," in *Works*, 4:219; "Fourth Chapter 2 Corinthians," in *Works*, 4:449–50; "Third Chapter Philippians," in *Works*, 5:83;. "Saint's Hiding-Place," in *Works*, 1:409–10; "Lydia," in *Works*, 6:523; "Breathing," in *Works*, 2:217. So Perkins, *Galatians*, 10, 43; *Hebrewes*, 31; *Work*, ed. Breward, 156–57. See Stoever, *passim*; Tipson's conclusion (315–41), which provides a careful critique of Pettit, among others.

107 "Divine Meditations," in *Works*, 7:189.

prepare hearts for salvation was "by the ministry of the gospel."[108] "Hearing begets seeing in religion. Death came in by the ear at the first. Adam hearing the serpent, that he should not have heard, death came in by the ear. So life comes in by the ear."[109] Preaching was the "chariot that carries Christ up and down the world. Christ doth not profit but as he is preached."[110] Thus "it is a gift of all gifts, the ordinance of preaching. God esteems it so, Christ esteems it so, and so should we esteem it."[111] Indeed, all the means of grace for conversion had to do with speech, which could confer the word of God, or drive home that which had been learned—"good company,"[112] conversations,[113] reading,[114] meditating,[115] and prayer.[116] This is not to suggest that the word invariably

---

108 "Description," in *Works*, 1:23–24; "Bowels Opened," in *Works*, 2:63; "Breathing," in *Works*, 2:216; "The Dead Man," in *Works*, 7:404.

109 "Excellency," in *Works*, 4:251–52; cf. "Fourth Chapter 2 Corinthians," in *Works*, 4:367, 377, 386; "Angels," in *Works*, 6:353; "Matchless Love," in *Works*, 6:409; "The Ruin of Mystical Jericho," in *Works*, 7:476; "Fruitful Labour," in *Works*, 6:380; "Lydia," in *Works*, 6:523; "Dead Man," in *Works*, 7:404–5; "Faith Triumphant," in *Works*, 7:434; "Divine Meditations," in *Works*, 7:198; Calvin, *Institutes*, 3.2.6, 3.2.31; Perkins, *Hebrewes*, 28; "Foundation," in *Work*, ed. Breward, 148, 161 (and *Workes*, 1:79); John Coolidge, *The Pauline Renaissance in England* (Oxford, England: Oxford University Press, 1970), 142. Cf. Calvin, *Institutes*, 3.2.6, 3.2.31. Q. Perkins, *Hebrewes*, 28; *Work*, ed. Breward, 161, 228.

110 "Fountain Opened," in *Works*, 5:508; cf. "Ungodly's Misery," in *Works*, 1:391; Perkins *Workes*, 1:71.

111 "Fountain Opened," in *Works*, 5:509.

112 "Bowels Opened," in *Works*, 2:166; "Matchless Love," in *Works*, 6:409.

113 "Returning Backslider," in *Works*, 2:355, 404; cf. "Third Chapter Philippians," in *Works*, 5:82.

114 "The Christian Work," in *Works*, 5:7.

115 "The Christian Work," in *Works*, 5:7; "Lydia," in *Works*, 6:530; "David's Conclusion," in *Works*, 7:90.

116 "David's Conclusion," in *Works*, 7:90.

wrought conversions; it too depended on the Spirit. "For if it were not the Spirit that persuaded the soul, when the minister speaks, alas! all ministerial persuasions are to no purpose."[117]

The sacraments are notably absent from the above list of means of grace for conversion; as he had with preaching, Sibbes warned against idolizing the sacraments, and further against assuming that "alway God gives grace with the sacraments."[118] The role of the sacraments was not as preparations for conversion[119] but rather to strengthen, confirm, or assure faith already present.

Conviction, though the beginning of true conversion, was also called a preparation.[120] Evoking what must have been a common image for conviction, Sibbes said, "A marvellous hard thing it is to bring a dull and a shifting heart to cry with feeling for mercy. Our hearts, like malefactors, until they be beaten from all shifts never cry for the mercy of the Judge."[121] Such despair was "the beginning of comfort; and trouble the

---

117 "Excellency," in *Works*, 4:219.

118 "First Chapter 2 Corinthians," in *Works*, 3:134.

119 Cf. "Returning Backslider," in *Works*, 2:379. Sibbes called the sacraments "means of salvation" in a list of other things in the church, including preaching, but that was in considering the entire Christian life (e.g., "Breathing," in *Works*, 2:232). On the other hand, it would have been surprising if he had called the sacrament a "means of *conversion*."

120 "Josiah," in *Works*, 6:33; "Third Chapter Philippians," in *Works*, 5:82; "Angels," in *Works*, 6:333; "Fountain Opened," in *Works*, 5:506; "Lydia," in *Works*, 6:522; "Rich Poverty," in *Works*, 6: 242–43; "Witness," in *Works*, 7:370; "Excellency," in *Works*, 4:219; "Fourth Chapter 2 Corinthians," in *Works*, 4:340, 368. Note, however, that this preparation was done by God. Cf. Preston, *Breast-Plate*, pt. i, 160–61.

121 "Bruised Reed," in *Works*, 1:44. cf. 47; "Rich Poverty," in *Works*, 6:243–44; "Soul's Conflict," in *Works*, 1:194. Cf. Perkins, "Foundation," in *Work*, ed. Breward, 156.

beginning of peace. A storm is the way to a calm, and hell the way to heaven."[122]

Sibbes assured his hearers that repentance would surely follow the Spirit's conviction.[123] "Let us labour to bring our hearts to wait in the use of the means, for God's good Spirit to enable me to see my state by nature, and to get out of it."[124] The exhortation to believe and repent, when answered by the heart, was the "spiritual echo and answer of the soul" that "comes from the Spirit of God in calling" and was initial conversion.[125] In that men could cooperate with God in this, "bruising," like hearing the Word, was both a state into which God brought them and a duty to be performed. "The paschal lamb was to be eaten with sour herbs; so Christ our passover must be eaten with repentance."[126] Once sin was bitter to the sinner, the Spirit would complete His preparatory work by the sinner's forsaking sin.

CONCLUSION

---

122 "Soul's Conflict," in *Works*, 1:158; Thomas Hooker, *The Soules Preparation* (London, 1638), 55. If the distinction between description and prescription is remembered, much (though not all) of the difference between Perkins and Hooker which Pettit and Kendall have suggested may be seen to vanish. Cf. Robert Horn, "Thomas Hooker—The Soul's Preparation for Christ," in *The Puritan Experiment in the New World* (London: Westminster Conference, 1976), 19–37; Stoever, 192–99.

123 "Excellency," in *Works*, 4:219.

124 "Angels," in *Works*, 6:354.

125 "Excellency," in *Works*, 4:219.

126 "Bowels Opened," in *Works*, 2:193; cf. "The Saint's Comforts," in *Works*, 6:171–72; "Lydia," in *Works*, 6:522.

The same means that Sibbes urged those in the covenant to use in order to be saved, he encouraged any Christian to use in order to become certain of their election or to grow in grace. "There are several ages in Christians. . . . Man, the perfectest creature, comes to perfection by little and little," Sibbes preached.[127] Therefore, most of his exhortations could and should have been appropriate to different groups of his hearers.

Aware that some believers constantly needed reassurance of God's graciousness, Sibbes exhorted them to continue to use the means of grace "in a continual dependence upon God." The Christian, no less than the unregenerate, was to say, "I will use these means, God may bless them; if not, I will trust him; he is not tied to the use of means, though I be."[128] Yet the use of means in preparation by the believer in no way meant that the Spirit did not prepare the heart: even as the Spirit initiated the covenant from before the creation of the world, so the initiative rested with God in both conversion and preparation.

The kind of exhortation for which Sibbes became known was particularly suited for his situation: preaching election and conversion within the framework of a covenant, practically and theologically. Practically, he preached to congregations who heard the Word so regularly that he could attend almost exclusively to pastoral issues. With apologetics largely unneeded, or relegated to a fraction of his hearers, Sibbes' sermons were

---

127 "Bruised Reed," in *Works*, 1:49.
128 "Saint's Hiding-Place," in *Works*, 1:421.

addressed to those who had been brought into the covenant as infants and kept in the covenant community, by convention or conviction. Either way, they would have been regularly present at the ministry of the Word and administration of the sacraments, and so were naturally inclined to have more gradual, less urgent religious lives. Theologically, Sibbes sermons fit well with the covenant framework. The line between the converted and the unconverted, clearer in churches that taught the coordination of baptism and regeneration, was blurred. There was, as a result, great scope in Sibbes' congregations for those who were certain of their obligation but agnostic of their fate. Sibbes preached that his hearers, by their baptism as infants and inclusion in the covenant community, had become particularly obliged to believe and live as Christians—but such was beyond their powers. This brought to the fore the gracious element in Christian theology, as Sibbes implored them with the electing love of God.

Sibbes' understanding of the nature of the covenant community explains his combination of Reformed theology and exhortation to means in conversion. Because of Sibbes' understanding of the covenant community, Sibbes could speak with certainty of the Holy Spirit's having "often knocked at their hearts, as willing to have kindled some holy desires in them."[129] Neither a higher estimation of human nature nor a belief in a prevenient grace enabled Sibbes to make such statements;

---

129 "Bruised Reed," in *Works*, 1:74.

instead, the fact that he preached in a context, and with an understanding of Christianity in which the concept of the covenant was widely accepted, gave him such license. Parents had taken on responsibilities for their children in baptism and religious training. Ministers did the same as they offered the Word to hearers week after week. As a result, to those within the covenanted community, preparation could appropriately be urged, yet not inconsistently with a thoroughly Reformed theology. Sibbes was not an unwitting representative of a nascent moralism; he was one of the last of the great Reformed preachers of England both to believe in theory and to know in practice an officially undivided covenant community.

CHAPTER FIVE

The Centrality
of the Heart

One reason why the Reformed foundations and covenantal framework of Richard Sibbes' theology may have been mistaken was his renowned passionate rhetoric.[1] A number of writers describe this affective element in Sibbes as "mysticism," though the term is usually undefined and often misunderstood, to the point "when practically any Christian who said his prayers affectively was a 'mystic.'"[2] This lack of definition

---

1   See G.F. Nuttall, *The Holy Spirit in Puritan Faith and Experience* (Oxford, England: Basil Blackwell, 1946), 14; William Haller, *The Rise of Puritanism* (New York: 1938), 163; Norman Pettit, *The Heart Prepared: Grace and Conversion in Puritan Spiritual Life* (New Haven, Conn.: Yale University Press, 1966), 66. Cf. U. Milo Kaufmann's judgment that "Richard Sibbes is one of the most attractive spirits among Puritan Divines of the seventeenth century" (*The Pilgrim's Progress and Traditions in Puritan Meditation* [New Haven, Conn.: Yale University Press, 1966], 141); John R. Knott Jr., *The Sword of the Spirit: Puritan Responses to the Bible* (Chicago: University of Chicago Press, 1980), 61.

2   Martin Thornton, *English Spirituality: An Outline of Ascetical Theology According to the English Pastoral Tradition* (London: Cowley, 1963), 13. Cf. David Knowles, *The English Mystical Tradition* (London: Burns and Oates, 1960), 2; Gordon S.

is present in most of the studies that have so presented Sibbes; nevertheless, something has often been seen as "mysticism" in Sibbes that has attracted these repeated comments. This chapter will explore Sibbes as a "mystic," suggesting that a more helpful adjective for understanding him would be the contemporary word "affectionate."

Sibbes himself used the word "mystical" sparingly; when he did, he intended essentially "mysterious," or something that contains a hidden knowledge.[3] More commonly he used the word "mystery,"[4] referring to the mysteries of the incarnation,[5] the church as the body of Christ,[6] the sacraments,[7] and allegorical or unclear passages of Scripture.[8] Negatively, he referred to the "mystery of popery"[9] (recalling the expression "mystery of iniquity" in 2 Thess. 2:7). Though "mystic" is little and vaguely used by Sibbes, this characterization is

Wakefield, "Mysticism and its Puritan Types," *London Quarterly and Holborn Review*, vol. XCXI, 6th series, XXXV (1966): 34.

3   "Divine Meditations," in *Works*, 7:200.

4   "Bowels Opened," in *Works*, 2:135, 168; "Bride's Longing," in *Works*, 6:542–43; "Art," in *Works*, 5:178; "Divine Meditations," in *Works*, 7:216, 220; "Excellency," in *Works*, 4:289; "Fountain Opened," in *Works*, 5:466–68, 471, 474–75, 482, 511. Geoffrey F. Nuttall has noted the common use of "mystical" as something more akin to "mysterious" in seventeenth-century religious writers (Nuttall, "Puritan and Quaker Mysticism," *Theology*, vol. LXXVIII [Oct. 1975]: 520).

5   "Fountain Opened," in *Works*, 5:482.

6   "Bowels Opened," in *Works*, 2:81; "Bride's Longing," in *Works*, 6:547; "Art," in *Works*, 5:192; "Christ's Suffering," in *Works*, 1:369; "Excellency," in *Works*, 4:242, 255, 264–65; "Fountain Opened," in *Works*, 5.464.

7   "Glorious Feast," in *Works*, 2:460–61.

8   "Bowels Opened," in *Works*, 2:137; "Fountain Opened," in *Works*, 5:513.

9   "Bowels Opened," in *Works*, 2:42–43; "Fountain Opened," in *Works*, 5:470–72, 475.

common enough to draw attention to his theological understanding of man.[10]

THE FACULTIES

The instrument upon which God's Spirit played is man, "a complicated structure of fluids and spirits, dust and eternal stuff."[11] As one trained in logic, Sibbes would have naturally tended toward describing man's faculties rather than analyzing them. Since Plato and Aristotle, the soul had been defined as being divided into various independent faculties or powers, each of which manages input and acts according to its own particular function. This view is known as "faculty psychology," and its most popular form conceived of the mind as consisting of three faculties: will, intellect, and emotions (or affections). Though Sibbes' own lifetime saw some of the biological advances (e.g. Harvey's discovery of the circulation of blood, Kepler's experiments on the eye) that helped to undermine the reigning "four humors" theory of physiology and faculty psychology, Sibbes appeared to know little or nothing of them. Thus, careful examination of Sibbes' understanding

---

10 On "mysticism" in Puritan religion, see Joe Lee Davis, "Mystical Versus Enthusiastic Sensibility," *Journal of the History of Ideas*, vol. IV/3 (June, 1943): 301–19; J.C. Brauer, "Puritan Mysticism and the Development of Liberalism," *Church History*, vol. XIX (1950): 151–70; Trinterud, "The Origins of Puritanism," *Church History*, vol. XX [1951]: 37–57; Maclear; Robert Middlekauff, "Piety and Intellect in Puritanism," *The William and Mary Quarterly*, 3rd series, vol. XXII/3 (July, 1965): 457–70; Wakefield; Nuttall, "Mysticism."

11 Cohen, 25.

of the human faculties brings to light a characteristic aspect of his theology that seems to attract his readers—the centrality of the affections.

Sibbes' presentation of faculty psychology presumed the following: the primary faculties of the soul are the senses, the imagination, the mind, and the heart, all intermixed with the bodily humors or fluids (blood, phlegm, yellow bile, and black bile); an excess or deficit of any of the humors would influence temperament and health. In order for the outward man to act, the inward man must unite in desire, willing the action of its parts. Once this is done, action would follow. This description presented man as both adequately unified to allow the culpability of the individual, yet complex enough to explain various actions individuals might take, as well as con-flicting attitudes toward, and motivations for, those actions. This is fundamental to understanding Sibbes' conceptions of depravity, conversion, and the further work of God in the soul.

By the word *soul* Sibbes meant the whole inner person. "Our body is but the case or tabernacle wherein our soul dwells; especially a man's self is his soul."[12] While the soul is in the body, its primary means of gaining information is through the physical senses.[13] The senses, in turn, are immedi-

---

12 "Saint's Hiding-Place," in *Works*, 1:408. Cf. Calvin's definition of soul: "an immor-tal yet created essence, which is his [man's] nobler part. Sometimes it is called 'spirit'" (*Institutes*, 1.15.2).

13 "Bowels Opened," in *Works*, 2:40; "Soul's Conflict," in *Works*, 1:178.

ately connected to the imagination, called the "phantasy"[14] or "opinion."[15] Here, the imagination is no more than a shallow understanding, reflecting the immediate reaction of the senses to pain or pleasure. So the imagination is the sensual judgment, naturally bypassing the rational judgment and directly stirring up the affections in the soul.[16] Though the soul was created "in that sweet harmony wherein there is no discord as an instrument in tune, fit to be moved to any duty,"[17] since the fall, the imagination has become the cause of much trouble in the soul.

This is not to suggest that the imagination had no positive use. "We should make our fancy serviceable to us in spiritual things," Sibbes taught. "And seeing God hath condescended to represent heavenly things to us under earthly terms, we should follow God's dealing herein. . . . A sanctified fancy will make every creature a ladder to heaven." After God has revealed His truth, it is the imagination's role to "colour divine truths, and make lightsome what faith believes."[18] For this reason, Sibbes' own sermons are replete with striking illustrations, such that one could almost reconstruct life in Stuart England from

---

14 "Bowels Opened," in *Works*, 2:40; cf. "Soul's Conflict," in *Works*, 1:137. The "imagination" or "phantasy" seems to be roughly equivalent to what would today be commonly spoken of as "feelings."

15 "Soul's Conflict," in *Works*, 1:178. Kaufmann calls Sibbes' discussion of the imagination in "The Soul's Conflict" "the first detailed engagement with the subject in seventeenth century Puritanism" (143).

16 "Soul's Conflict," in *Works*, 1:179–82.

17 "Soul's Conflict," in *Works*, 1:173.

18 "Soul's Conflict," in *Works*, 1:185.

Sibbes' sermons alone. Everything, from the "Gloria Patri" in church to blind men on the streets, from military tactics to the Englishman's view of far-off places, was used by Sibbes to capture the imaginations of his hearers and to "make our fancy serviceable to us in spiritual things."

In contrast, the role of the "mind,"[19] "judgment,"[20] or "understanding,"[21] located in the brain,[22] is to take in the information from the senses through the imagination—and by means of rational discourse—to determine what is true. In choosing what it perceives to be the true, the understanding shows wisdom or foolishness.[23] This faculty is the image of God in the soul and therefore separates humans from beasts.[24] So, while *soul* is usually used to mean the entire inner person, Sibbes occasionally used it to mean that part of man unique to him among the creatures: the understanding.[25] Though its proper function is to give decisive reasons and thoughts to the heart, ruling the soul,[26] in the unregenerated man the

---

19 "Breathing," in *Works*, 2:218.

20 "Bowels Opened," in *Works*, 2:92; "Bruised Reed," in *Works*, 1:83; "Soul's Conflict," in *Works*, 1:178.

21 "Breathing," in *Works*, 2:218–19, 221, 227, 237–38; "Bride's Longing," in *Works*, 6:544; "Bruised Reed," in *Works*, 1:83; "Soul's Conflict," in *Works*, 1:178, 246; "Saint's Safety," in *Works*, 1:297.

22 "Breathing," in *Works*, 2:218, 227; "Bride's Longing," in *Works*, 6:544.

23 "Breathing," in *Works*, 2:221, "Soul's Conflict," in *Works*, 1:246; see also "Angels," in *Works*, 6:328. Cf. Thomas Adams, *Mysticall Bedlam* (London: 1629), 493.

24 "Breathing," in *Works*, 2:216, 227. On the image of God in fallen humanity, see "Faithful Covenanter," in *Works*, 6:220; "First Chapter 2 Corinthians," in *Works*, 3:40, 135; cf. "Excellency," in *Works*, 4:267.

25 "Soul's Conflict," in *Works*, 1:245.

26 "Breathing," in *Works*, 2:218; "Bowels Opened," in *Works*, 2:9; "Saint's Safety," in *Works*, 1:297.

understanding, "since the fall, until it hath a higher light and strength, yieldeth to our imagination" and to "bribes" from the unsubdued will working in conjunction with the imagination.[27]

THE CENTRALITY OF THE HEART

It is not Sibbes' statements of the supreme place of reason in the soul that are remarkable; rather, what strikes the reader is his affectionate language.[28] For Sibbes, Christianity is a love story: God is essentially a husband to His people: "with the same love that God loves Christ, he loves all his."[29] "You see how full of love he was. What drew him from heaven to earth, and so to his cross and to his grave, but love to mankind?"[30] In fact, "Religion," Sibbes said, "is mainly in the affections."[31] God is the affectionate, loving sovereign, with every "sincere Christian . . . a favourite."[32] Given this understanding of Christianity, it is not surprising that Sibbes published sermons on the Song of Solomon; the book's erotic poetry expressed well "the mutual joys and mutual praises of Christ and his

---

27 "Bruised Reed," in *Works*, 1:83; "Breathing," in *Works*, 2:221.

28 E.g., Richard Baxter included Sibbes high on his list of "Affectionate Practical English writiers" which even the poorest student's library should include (Richard Baxter, *A Christian Directory, Or, A Summ of Practical Theology and Cases of Conscience* [London: 1673], 922).

29 "Description," in *Works*, 1:12; cf. "Excellency," in *Works*, 4:242.

30 "Excellency," in *Works*, 4:262.

31 "Returning Backslider," in *Works*, 2:368.

32 "Yea and Amen," in *Works*, 4:131.

church."[33] Sibbes realized that sensual language is a powerful metaphor for the love between God and the soul.

"The putting of lively colours upon common truths hath oft a strong working both upon the fancy and our will and affections,"[34] and it was the will and affections, Sibbes said, that must be reached by the preacher. "By heart I mean, especially, the will and affections."[35] As the understanding is in the brain, so the will, affections, and desires are in the heart. Thus Sibbes often used the four words interchangably.[36] The heart is the faculty to which the understanding gives its thoughts and reasons "as a prince doth his wiser subjects, and as counsellors do a well ordered state."[37] The heart, in turn, affects the understanding. Sibbes spoke of the heart as essentially revealing the person.[38] Though the heart, or will, always chooses "with the advisement of reason,"[39] it is the heart, not reason, that is the determining (not judging) faculty of the soul,[40] particularly in the unregenerate man. It is the "fountain

---

33 "Bowels Opened," in *Works*, 2:5. Cf. "This book is nothing else but a plain demonstration and setting forth of the love of Christ to his church, and of the love of the church to Christ," ("Spouse," in *Works*, 2:200).

34 "Soul's Conflict," in *Works*, 1:184.

35 "Matchless Love," in *Works*, 6:403.

36 "Bride's Longing," in *Works*, 6:544; "Breathing," in *Works*, 2:218, 227; "Bruised Reed," in *Works*, 1:83; "Soul's Conflict," in *Works*, 1:179–80, 184; "Josiah," in *Works*, 6:31; "Church's Visitation," in *Works*, 1:374. So too Perkins (e.g., 562–63) and John Preston (e.g., *Breast-Plate,* pt. i, 86–87).

37 "Soul's Conflict," in *Works*, 1:245.

38 "Breathing," in *Works*, 2:219. Cf. Calvin, *Institutes*, 3.6.4.

39 "Excellency," in *Works*, 4:225

40 "Breathing," in *Works*, 2:221.

of life,"[41] the "inward motion," the "feet," the "wind" of the soul.[42] Therefore, Sibbes said, "Love is the weight and wing of the soul, which carries it where it goes."[43]

IN DEPRAVITY

Sibbes presented even depravity in affectionate terms. All non-Christians, he said, are "hard-hearted";[44] before conversion, all are "full of malice and base affections."[45] The carnal heart, overcast with passion and strong affections to the world, hates God naturally and cherishes corruption and rebellion against Him.[46]

According to Sibbes, the heart's preeminence is not a result of the fall but is central to God's design.[47] Yet, Sibbes recognized that problems occur where the heart or will is unsubdued; in such souls, the will usurps the rightful role of the understanding, where "the heart being corrupt sets the wit awork, to satisfy corrupt will."[48] Thus, both the heart and the

---

41 "Breathing," in *Works*, 2:227.

42 "Breathing," in *Works*, 2:218, 227; "Soul's Conflict," in *Works*, 1:159.

43 "Bowels Opened," in *Works*, 2:129.

44 "Soul's Conflict," in *Works*, 1:177.

45 "Breathing," in *Works*, 2:234. Cf. Calvin's statement that "our heart especially inclines by its own natural instinct toward unbelief," (*Institutes*, 3.3.20).

46 "Angels," in *Works*, 6:342; "Bride's Longing," in *Works*, 6:540; "Demand," in *Works*, 7:487; "Fountain Opened," in *Works*, 5:471.

47 "Soul's Conflict," in *Works*, 1:159; cf. "Privileges," in *Works*, 5:276; "Church's Visitation," in *Works*, 1:374.

48 "Soul's Conflict," in *Works*, 1:145; cf. "Bruised Reed," in *Works*, 1:83; "Breathing," in *Works*, 2:221; "Divine Meditations," in *Works*, 7:194.

understanding are dealt with in conversion and sanctification, the heart being the goal but judgment always being the entry point.[49] As a result, the role of the understanding is to "breed" and "lead," to "work upon," to "warm" and "kindle" and even "inflame" the affections.[50] Reason, Sibbes said, "is a beam of God."[51]

On the other hand, Sibbes was not content with religion contained entirely in the brain; he scorned men that "never see spiritual things experimentally . . . though they know these things in the brain."[52] "A man knows no more in religion than he loves and embraceth with the affections of his soul."[53] To embrace something in one's affections was to know it experimentally, because the "will is the carriage of the soul."[54] If the grace of Christ were effectually working in the heart, one would do good; on the other hand, to be warned about evil desires and yet persist in pursuing them is "atheism" in the heart.[55]

---

49 "Breathing," in *Works*, 2:218–19; "Bruised Reed," in *Works*, 1:83; "Divine Meditations," in *Works*, 7:200–201; "Saint's Hiding-Place," in *Works*, 1:419.

50 "Angels," in *Works*, 6:334, "Breathing," in *Works*, 2:218–19; "Excellency," in *Works*, 4:271; "Privileges," in *Works*, 5:282; "Soul's Conflict," in *Works*, 1:201, 245.

51 "Excellency," in *Works*, 4:234; cf. "Fountain Opened," in *Works*, 5:467. Cf. Nutall, *Holy Spirit*, 35–37.

52 "Divine Meditations," in *Works*, 7:200–201.

53 "Fountain Opened," in *Works*, 5:478.

54 "Breathing," in *Works*, 2:218–19.

55 "Church's Riches," in *Works*, 4:524; "Soul's Conflict," in *Works*, 1:174–75.

In Conversion

Conversion must, then, take place in the heart. Though it must include sanctification of judgment, it must also include the subduing of the will.[56] "For it is not knowledge that will bring to heaven, for the devil hath that, but it is knowledge sanctified, seizing upon the affections."[57] In the unconverted man, the heart or will runs roughshod over the understanding, bribing it and bringing it along with its carnal desires. In conversion, both the mind and the heart need to be changed—the mind is enlightened, and the very desires and tastes of the heart are altered.[58] God must come in to the heart to rule it,[59] seizing on the powers of the soul, subduing the inward rising of the heart and the innate rebellion against the truth of God; He must "bring the heart down"[60] by opening the heart to believe, and working in it to cause repentance.[61] God "turns" the heart to Himself and "frees the will" to serve Him.[62] Though the whole man remains touched

---

56 "Breathing," in *Works*, 2:218.
57 "Breathing," in *Works*, 2:240.
58 "Returning Backslider," in *Works*, 2:416; "Breathing," in *Works*, 2:220, 222; "Description," in *Works*, 1:24; "Privileges," in *Works*, 5:284; "Bride's Longing," in *Works*, 6:541; "Excellency," in *Works*, 4:221; "Faithful Covenanter," in *Works*, 6:19; "Soul's Conflict," in *Works*, 1:268; "Divine Meditations," in *Works*, 7:199; "To the Christian Reader," "Exposition of the Creed," in *Works*, 1xlii; "Bowels Opened," in *Works*, 2:173.
59 "Bride's Longing," in *Works*, 6:551.
60 "Bride's Longing," in *Works*, 6:540.
61 "Yea and Amen," in *Works*, 4:122; "Art," in *Works*, 5:190.
62 "Knot of Prayer," in *Works*, 7:251; "Pattern," in *Works*, 7:511.

by the fall, the enlightened understanding will increasingly judge correctly and will be obeyed rather than coerced, allowing man to show his distinction from the beasts. In Sibbes, then, both depravity and conversion find their core in the heart, but neither in such a way as to deny the essential role of the understanding.

Therefore, while Sibbes taught that the will or heart is the most powerful faculty in the soul, that it must be changed at conversion, and that the understanding will never move the soul without the will, he never presented religion as essentially arational: "All grace come in through the understanding enlightened."[63] The mind is "the most excelleant part of the soul."[64] The purpose of regeneration is to "reestablish" the "ideal supremacy of reason over will."[65] In the regenerate man, the Spirit of God subdues the will to His Word coming through the understanding: "All comfort cometh into the soul by knowledge. . . . Indeed, all graces are nothing but knowledge digested."[66] If to be a mystic, or "experiential," is fundamentally to exalt the role of the heart above that of the mind, then the term does not apply to Sibbes.

---

63 "Excellency," in *Works*, 4:258–59; cf. "Soul's Conflict," in *Works*, 1:245; "Description," in *Works*, 1:24.

64 "Angels," in *Works*, 6:334.

65 Miller, 260.

66 "Fourth Chapter 2 Corinthians," in *Works*, 4:459; cf. "Bruised Reed," in *Works*, 1:83.

In Motivation

Given the centrality of the heart in Sibbes' presentations of depravity and conversion, it is no surprise to find him speaking of the Christian life as one driven by holy loves and desires. "The gospel breeds love in us to God," he said.[67] Though this love may first be simply for the salvation Christ has brought, "when she [the soul] is brought to him, and finds that sweetness that is in him, then she loves him for himself."[68] God becomes the one thing the soul most desires. Echoing Augustine's *Confessions*, Sibbes wrote, "The soul is never quiet till it comes to God . . . and that is the one thing the soul desireth."[69] Only those who so love God, preferring Him to carnal pleasures, riches, and honors, find Him.[70] A desire to do all to honor God and love Him typifies the life of the Christian.[71] "Whatsoever we do else, if it be not stirred by the Spirit, apprehending the love of God in Christ, it is but morality. What are all our performances if they be not out of love to God?"[72]

For the Christian, to be in this world means separation from what he most desires. Christ Himself underwent this

---

67 "Description," in *Works*, 1:24.

68 "Divine Meditations," in *Works*, 7:217.

69 "Breathing," in *Works*, 2:217–18.

70 "Description," in *Works*, 1:24; "Spouse," in *Works*, 2:204; "Breathing," in *Works*, 2:222.

71 "Breathing," in *Works*, 2:220; "Excellency," in *Works*, 4:271.

72 "Description," in *Works*, 1:24.

during the incarnation.[73] Therefore, Christians, too, must expect this life to be marked by longing. Like David, the Christian will desire "to see the beauty of God in his house, that his soul might be ravished in the excellency of the object, and that the hightest powers of his soul, his understanding, will, and affections might be fully satisfied, that he might have full contentment."[74] "Therefore, we should press the heart forward to God"[75] because the Christian will only find rest in heaven, "where all desires shall be accomplished."[76] Affectionately stated, the point of the Christian life is "to grow in nearer communion with God by his Spirit, to have more knowledge and affection, more love and joy and delight in the best things daily."[77] Therefore, Christians are to "labour to have great affections" for God, and subsequently, for other, lesser goods, particularly His ordinances through which His presence is enjoyed.[78] Whereas the worldling must always finally loose that which he desires, the Christian never does.[79]

Preeminently, the affection God uses is love. Once one is converted, this love becomes the driving force of the soul to

---

73 "Fountain Opened," in *Works*, 5:533.

74 "Breathing," in *Works*, 2:237–38.

75 "Soul's Conflict," in *Works*, 1:202.

76 "Breathing," in *Works*, 2:227–29.

77 "Breathing," in *Works*, 2:247.

78 "Fountain Opened," in *Works*, 5:478; "Returning Backslider," in *Works*, 2:266; "Breathing," in *Works*, 2:229; "Bowels Opened," in *Works*, 2:157; "Glorious Feast," in *Works*, 2:481.

79 "The Danger of Backsliding," in *Works*, 7:413.

God. As the "prime and leading affection of the soul,"[80] the "firstborn affection of the soul,"[81] love motivates the soul to action. "Love is an affection full of inventions," zealously pursuing the pleasure of the beloved.[82] Thus, love "will constrain us to obedience"[83] because "it studies to please the person loved as much as it can every way."[84] That is why Sibbes exhorted: "Beloved, get love. . . . It melts us into the likeness of Christ. It constrains, it hath a kind of holy violence in it. No water can quench it. We shall glory in sufferings for that we love. Nothing can quench that holy fire that is kindled from heaven. It is a glorious grace."[85] Similarly, love performs a "sweet kind of tyranny" making a man willing even to die.[86] "Nothing is hard to love; it carries all the powers of the soul with it."[87] Thus, since one who loves will do anything for "the contentation of the person beloved,"[88] one should "labour for a spirit of love. . . . Nothing is grievous to the person that loves."[89]

Furthermore, since love "stirs up the soul to make out for" the beloved, the love for God has as its end, not only the pleasure of the beloved, but "union and fellowship with the person

---

80 "Soul's Conflict," in *Works*, 1:130.
81 "Sword," in *Works*, 1:105.
82 "Soul's Conflict," in *Works*, 1:181; "Excellency," in *Works*, 4:274–75; "Sword," in *Works*, 1:116.
83 "Danger," in *Works*, 7:411.
84 "Excellency," in *Works*, 4:271.
85 "Excellency," in *Works*, 4:274–75; "Divine Meditations," in *Works*, 7:221.
86 "Art," in *Works*, 5:182; cf. "Description," in *Works*, 1:9.
87 "Soul's Conflict," in *Works*, 1:279.
88 "Privileges," in *Works*, 5:276–77.
89 "Difficulty," in *Works*, 1:399.

we affect."[90] Therefore the Christian has "this further desire of familiarity with Christ" and yearns for "further inward kisses of his love."[91] Love leaves one at rest only in the beloved.[92] "Love is an affection of union. What we love . . . we are knit unto."[93]

Thus, "the more loving Christian ever the more humble Christian."[94] Yet Sibbes did not infer from this a divinely sanctioned asceticism; though self-love can be "a common corruption that cleaves to the nature of all men,"[95] there is also a self-love that "God hath put in us . . . not sinful, but love of preserving our nature."[96] This instinct for self-preservation, or "self-love," causes people to care for themselves, both physically and spiritually. So, man grows spiritually by both love of God and a godly love of self.

In Assurance

Sibbes taught that the examination of the heart is essential to indicate the state of the soul, because "there is nothing that charcteriseth and sets a stamp upon a Christian so much as desires. All other things may be counterfeit. Words and

---

90 "Privileges," in *Works*, 5:276–77.
91 "Spouse," in *Works*, 2:205.
92 "Privileges," in *Works*, 5:276–77.
93 "Judgment," in *Works*, 4:98.
94 "Privileges," in *Works*, 5:281–82.
95 "Soul's Conflict," in *Works*, 1:177.
96 "Returning Backslider," in *Works*, 2:266.

actions may be counterfeit, but the desires and affections cannot, because they are the immediate issues and productions of the soul."[97] The heart is the only place the Christian can examine "for the evidence of our good estate in religion. Let us not so much search what Christ hath done, but search our own hearts how we have engaged ourselves to God in Christ, that we believe and witness our believeing, that we lead a life answerable to our faith, renounce all but Christ."[98] Without affections, a "man . . . is like *mare mortuum,* the dead sea that never stirreth";[99] "for it is affection that makes a Christian."[100]

The brain cannot give convincing witness to conversion, because religion can be known to the understanding yet a stranger in the heart.[101] As Sibbes observed from the "back-sliding" of Demas, "we are not as we know, but as we love."[102] The Christian's assurance will never be greater than his love. "Therefore, when we find our heart inflamed with love to God,

---

97 "Breathing," in *Works,* 2:219. See also "Breathing," in *Works,* 2:220–21; "Bowels Opened," in *Works,* 2:129; "Danger," in *Works,* 7:413; "Privileges," in *Works,* 5:282; "Pattern," in *Works,* 7:514–15; "Returning Backslider," in *Works,* 2:264; "Saint's Hiding-Place," in *Works,* 1:419. "We may dissemble words and actions, but we cannot dissemble our desires and affections; we may paint fire, but we cannot paint heat. Therefore God judgeth us more by our desires and affections than by our words and actions" ("Bride's Longing," 6:543). Cf. William Perkins' suggestion of gaining assurance through sanctification of the heart because "we knowe it sufficiently to be true, and not painted fire, if there be heate, though there be no flame" (*The Whole Treatise of the Cases of Conscience* [Cambridge, England: 1606], 77*).*

98 "Demand," in *Works,* 7:483; "Bowels Opened," in *Works,* 2:123; "Judgment," in *Works,* 4:101–2.

99 "Returning Backslider," in *Works,* 2:368.

100 "Faithful Covenanter," in *Works,* 6:10,12.

101 "Divine Meditations," in *Works,* 7:200–201.

102 "Danger of Backsliding," in *Works,* 7:412; cf. "Glance of Heaven," in *Works,* 4:182.

we may know that God hath shined upon our souls in the pardon of sin; and proportionably to our measure of love is our assurance of pardon. Therefore we should labour for a greater measure thereof, that our hearts may be the more inflamed in the love of God."[103] Furthermore, affections testify not only of one's conversion but also of one's sanctification: "If a man ask, how I know that I am sanctified? the answer must be, I believe, I know it to be so. The work of working these things in me comes of God; but the work of discerning them is certain, how our affection stands in this case—comes of us."[104]

IN BACKSLIDING

While affections for God characterize a Christian, Sibbes recognized they are not the only desires in a Christian's heart. Even the best Christian should know that "if we would examine ourselves . . . it would bring us on our knees, and make our faces be confounded, to consider what a deal of atheism there is in our heart . . . that must be mortified and subdued."[105] Worldly-mindedness "will glue thy affections to the earth," Sibbes warned, "and will not suffer them to be lifted up to Christ."[106] This is why those with fewer worldly goods often

---

103 "Returning Backslider," in *Works*, 2:264.

104 "Witness," in *Works*, 7:377.

105 "Faithful Covenanter," in *Works*, 6:11; cf. "Danger," in *Works*, 7:409; "Angels," in *Works*, 6:332; "Knot of Prayer," in *Works*, 7:248; "Christ's Suffering," in *Works*, 1:364; "Right Receiving," in *Works*, 4:62–63; "Soul's Conflict," in *Works*, 1:171; "Judgment," in *Works*, 4:86–87.

106 "Spouse," in *Works*, 2:205–6.

have "more loving souls" and are more "heated with affection." Having less at stake in this world, "a poor Christian cares not for cold disputes. Instead of that he loves; and that is the reason why a poor soul goes to heaven with more joy whilst others are entangled."[107] So, "the life of a Christian should be a meditation how to unloose his affections from inferior things. He will easily die that is dead before in affection. . . . He that is much in heaven in his thoughts is free from being tossed with tempests here below."[108]

Sibbes knew the freedom of affections he preached: as he lay dying, Sibbes was reportedly asked, "how hee (Dr. Sips) did in his soule?" to which he replied, "I should doe God much wrong if I should not say very well."[109]

Yet a peaceful demise was not the certain earthly end of the Christian. Sibbes' frequent references to the wanderings of Christian hearts shows that real danger lies even for the converted; the danger of backsliding is as much an affair of the heart as is growth in grace. The affections are always ready to rebel and—once in rebellion, and joined by Satan—to increase their revolt.

A "double heart" is particularly dangerous because "it will regard God no longer than it can enjoy that which it joins

---

107 "Divine Meditations," in *Works*, 7:194–95.

108 "Soul's Conflict," in *Works*, 1:164, cf. 159, 163, 286; "Bowels Opened," in *Works*, 2:186; "Providence," in *Works*, 5:42; "Christ is Best," in *Works*, 1:341; "Privileges," in *Works*, 5:283; "First Chapter 2 Corinthians," in *Works*, 3:208. Cf. Calvin, *Institutes*, 2.9.1.

109 Hartlib, *Ephemerides*, 1635.

together with him."[110] The division of affections is a mark
of an unconverted heart, and it is changed at conversion.[111]
The devil may be contented with half the heart, but Christ
"will not have it so."[112] Therefore, the Christian should "take
heed of the pleasures of the world, lest they drown thy soul,
as they do the souls of many that profess themselves to be
Christians."[113]

Sibbes taught that, if love is the light of life, then love of
darkness becomes a blinding affection[114]—yet even in those
blinded for a time, there may be "a secret love of Christ." If so,
the "pulses will beat this way, and good affections will discover
themselves"[115] because "his heart is fixed."[116] "Whatsoever we
give the supremacy of the inward man to, whatsoever we love
most, whatsoever we trust most, whatsoever we fear most,
whatsoever we joy and delight most, whatsoever we obey
most—that is our god."[117] In the end, one's love indicates one's
God[118]—for no human lives without loving.[119]

---

110 "Soul's Conflict," in *Works*, 1:218–19.
111 "Breathing," in *Works*, 2:218. "Grace confines the soul to one thing," "Breathing," in *Works*, 2:217.
112 "Spouse," in *Works*, 2:205–6; "Returning Backslider," in *Works*, 2:261.
113 "Spouse," in *Works*, 2:205–6.
114 "Spouse," in *Works*, 2:205–6.
115 "Bowels Opened," in *Works*, 2:48.
116 "Two Sermons," in *Works*, 7:355–56. Cf. Preston, *Breast-Plate*, pt. iii, 215.
117 "Faithful Covenanter," in *Works*, 6:12.
118 "Soul's Conflict," in *Works*, 1:268; "Saint's Safety," in *Works*, 1:298.
119 "Privileges," in *Works*, 5:281–82.

In Sanctification

Finally, as depravity, conversion, backsliding, and assurance are all affairs of the heart, so too is sanctification: one grows by means of one's affections. One should "labour therefore to know the world, that thou mayest detest it. In religion, the more we know the more we will love; but all the worldly things, the more we know the less we will affect them. . . . The more we know the vanities of the world and the excellencies of grace, the more we will love the one and hate the other."[120]

By meditating on the things of religion—and the things of the world—one will grow appropriate affections for each. Fundamental is the believer's decision to "plough up their own hearts."[121] Sibbes said that God will "have us take words unto ourselves, for exciting of the graces of God in us by words, blowing up of the affections, and for manifestation of the hidden man of the heart."[122] Such action will ensure that Christ is made "sweet . . . to the soul."[123] Realizing that the affection is particularly stirred by sight,[124] one must labor to "see spiritual things experimentally."[125] This is why examples of men are so useful to the believer, because examples work most on

---

120 "Danger," in *Works*, 7:413.

121 "Church's Visitation," in *Works*, 1:382.

122 "Returning Backslider," in *Works*, 2:260.

123 "Judgment," in *Works*, 4:92.

124 "Breathing," in *Works*, 2:243, 237; "Divine Meditations," in *Works*, 7:203–4; "Excellency," in *Works*, 4:251; "Fountain Opened," in *Works*, 5:478.

125 "Divine Meditations," in *Works*, 7:200–201.

the affections.[126] Most of all then, the believer should look to Christ: "When we look upon the mercy of God in Christ, it kindleth love, and love kindleth love, as fire kindleth fire";[127] "let us try our love by our labouring for that sight of Christ which we may have."[128]

Preaching—especially affectionate preaching—is preeminently the means to grow such loving affections. According to Sibbes, this is preaching in which "Christ [was] truly laid open to the hearts of people . . . the knowledge and preaching of Christ in his state and offices."[129] "Indeed, 'preaching' is the ordinance of God, sanctified for the begetting of faith, for the opening of the understanding, for the drawing of the will and affections to Christ. . . . Therefore, as we esteem faith and all the good we have by it, let us be stirred up highly to prize and esteem of this ordinance of God."[130] Because Sibbes taught that "God has opened His heart to us in His Word,"[131] it follows that "those ages wherein the Spirit of God is most, is where Christ is most preached,"[132] and "where the ordinances of Christ are held forth with life and power, they have more

---

126 "Christian's Work," in *Works*, 5:122–23; cf. 124; "Divine Meditations," in *Works*, 7:193.
127 "Excellency," in *Works*, 4:271.
128 "Spouse," in *Works*, 2:205.
129 "Description," in *Works*, 1:24.
130 "Fountain Opened," in *Works*, 5:514–15.
131 "Soul's Conflict," in *Works*, 1:212.
132 "Description," in *Works*, 1:24.

heavenly and enlarged affections than others have, as the experience of Christians will testify."[133]

While preaching is preeminent, other means are also encouraged upon the believer. Though individual study and meditation are never to be substitutes for preaching in stirring the affections, the Christian has an obligation to "soar much aloft in our meditations, and see the excellencies of Christ."[134] As in conversion the gospel must proceed from the understanding into the heart if it is to be effective, so too "comfortable" thoughts must so proceed if they are to be useful.[135] In addition, Sibbes exhorted the believer to the "lifting up the heart to God,"[136] since "what he desires as a Christian, he prays for, and what he prays for he desires."[137] Prayers that do not reflect the true desires of the heart are hypocrisy, not true prayers.[138] Finally, as it is the heart that leads the Christian to fellowship with God, it is the heart also that leads to fellowship with other believers, which—like the other means—stirs up further affections for God.[139]

---

133 "Bowels Opened," in *Works*, 2:161.

134 "Danger," in *Works*, 7:409. Cf. 413; "Returning Backslider," in *Works*, 2:260; "Divine Meditations," in *Works*, 7:189.

135 "Two Sermons," in *Works*, 7:355–56. These were the last words of which we have evidence that Sibbes spoke publicly. He died within the week.

136 "Fountain Opened," in *Works*, 5:469.

137 "Breathing," in *Works*, 2:222; "Bride's Longing," in *Works*, 6:540.

138 "Knot of Prayer," in *Works*, 7:248.

139 "Bowels Opened," in *Works*, 2:161; "Bride's Longing," in *Works*, 6:541–42; "Description," in *Works*, 1:14.

CONCLUSION

In his affectionate language, it becomes clear that Sibbes moved concerns of Christian piety inward,[140] affirming that it is actually love that is the root of all good and of all evil:

> We must know it is not the world simply that draws our heart from God and goodness, but the love of the world. Worldly things are good in themselves, and given to sweeten our passage to heaven. . . . Use it as a servant all thy days, and not as a master, and thou mayest have comfort therein. It is not the world properly that hurts us, but our setting our hearts upon it; whenas God should be in our thoughts, our spirits are even drunk with the cares below. . . . This world and the things thereof are all good, and were all made of God for the benefit of his creature, did not our immoderate affection make them hurtful, which indeed embitters every sweet unto us. This is the root of all evil.[141]

Warning against deliberate hypocrisy as well as foolish pride, Sibbes radically interiorized Christianity. This inward piety was not seen primarily in an overriding concern for "union experiences" with God, which are often considered the

---

140 Haller, 209.
141 "Danger," in *Works*, 7:412–13. Cf. Calvin, *Institutes*, 3.9.3–4.

hallmark of mysticism. Such a concern, if it is intended to imply spirituality divorced from rationality or an antinomian ethic, is not at all present in Sibbes. However, if one simply means that "wherever there is conjoined with serious Christianity a certain tenderness of heart and a hunger and thirst for God, and the metaphors of Scripture are believed to enshrine definite promise of intimate communion with Him, we are not wrong to speak of Mysticism,"[142] then Sibbes could be classified as a mystic. Perhaps it would be better to speak of the "tender lyricism barely controllable" that is evident in his sermons.[143] In the end, whether the inwardness that marks Sibbes should be termed "mysticism" is a matter more important to a study of mysticism than of Sibbes.

Noting Sibbes' "affectionate" theology is important for an accurate understanding of him and his preaching. His understanding of the human psyche necessitates heavy emphasis on saving knowledge settling in the heart and reflected in experience and practice. In a united heart, the affections affect, the desires desire, the will wills. The heart and the understanding are united, and the heart stirs up the bodily humors to pursue what it has perceived as good. The humors obey the will, and the outward members work to attain the thing desired. Thus, when the object desired is true and good, the soul is united in desiring it, and attainment brings happiness, contentment, and satisfaction. When the object is neither true nor good,

---

142 Wakefield, 45.
143 Nuttall, "Mysticism," 527.

then there is disruption in the soul and a lack of contentment even in attainment.

A theology of man that cemented the relation between the belief of the heart and the action of the members was particularly appropriate in Sibbes' ecclesiastical and sociopolitical environment. Each person was understood as a microcosm: the senses, imagination, heart, and members are all spoken of as desiring; the imagination, understanding, and heart are all capable of some kind of judgment. It resembles a governing elite, with the council of advisers (the understanding) advising the more powerful ruler (the heart) commanding the lower members. Sibbes described the inner man as "the consistory of the soul."[144] The wise ruler listens to his advisers, particularly when they counsel with God's Word, and works in accord with them. The evil ruler attempt to subvert the judgment of his counselors and works apart from and against them. With this understanding of man, preaching must be the salvific ordinance and, to discover its health, a well-run kingdom should look to its "faithful ministers"—"the pillars of this tottering world."[145]

---

144 "Soul's Conflict," in *Works*, 1:289.

145 "Providence," in *Works*, 5:50. Note his strong statements on this subject in "First Chapter 2 Corinthians," in *Works*, 3:279–80 (not published until twenty years after his death).

CHAPTER SIX

Assurance
of Salvation

R ichard Sibbes can easily be taken to be an exponent of the tendency of many in the 1620s and 1630s to become to become more inward-looking in matters of religion,"[1] regardless of social implications or public interest. As he said, "we should have a double eye: one eye to see that which is amiss in us, our own imperfections, thereby to carry ourselves in a perpetual humility; but another eye of faith, to see what we have in Christ, our perfection in him."[2] This "eye of faith" was crucial for a godly preacher like Sibbes, and not merely for reasons of personal piety.

A kind of spiritual second sight that could see that God was at work was essential for assurance of salvation; yet this eye

---

1   Cliffe, *The Puritan Gentry*, 198; cf. Perry Miller, *The New England Mind: The Seventeenth Century* (New York: Harvard University Press, 1939), 55.

2   "Bowels Opened," in *Works*, 2:85; cf. 136; "Divine Meditations," in *Works*, 7:187; "First Chapter 2 Corinthians," in *Works*, 3:448–49. Calvin, *Institutes*, 3.2.25.

of faith was not only turned inward; it also saw God's hand at work in the world and, most importantly, in the church. It was particularly important to a minister such as Sibbes, in Conforming: the same uneasy balance of piety, patience, and passion was to characterize the believer's internal religious quest—whether to find assurance, draw comfort, discern providence, or educate conscience.

This chapter will examine Sibbes' understanding of assurance, which is a central feature of his preaching, exploring its significance in understanding Sibbes' ability to remain within the Church of England. In so doing, this chapter will clarify the issue of Sibbes' Conformity, as his concern for inward piety is shown to have been that which allowed his continuing Conformity rather than being an avenue to Nonconformity.

ASSURANCE

Comfort, of course, comes most of all from assurance of one's salvation.[3] Sermonic rhetoric about this doctrine can be quite equivocal, intending to assure the doubting believer that his election was based on nothing in himself and that his perseverance is assured by the same God who began a good work in him (Phil 1:6), and in the next moment exhorting believers to make sure their interest in Christ.

Whatever rush of certainty may have attended the initial

---

3   "Jubilee," in *Works*, 5:244.

preaching of the Protestant gospel, by the early seventeenth century (if not before), such preaching often generated confusion in its hearers. If sincere confusion could arise in the hearts of earnest listeners in the early seventeenth century, it can creep much more easily into the modern reader's discussion of assurance or certainty. The combination of confusion with controversies (then and now) only serves to make examining Sibbes' treatment of assurance more arduous. To understand more clearly Sibbes' words, the tradition in which he preached must be presented.

Any discussion on assurance that is unclear in the object of assurance can hardly be expected to be clear on any other matter. It is vital to know whether one is discussing the objective assurance of faith—that Christ is all He professes to be and will freely save whoever believes in Him—or the subjective assurance of faith, in which one is assured of one's own salvation.[4] The former use was prominent in the century after the Reformation, particularly in anti-Roman polemics.[5] The latter emphasis, though always present in the Reformed tradition, became more clearly distinguished and prominent in the English church due to the increased attention given to pastoral issues as the Protestant succession from Elizabeth to James seemed more certain. This distinction is essential in

---

4   For a brief, accurate, systematic distinction of these two, see Louis Berkhof, *Systematic Theology* (Grand Rapids, Mich.: 1939), 507–9.

5   Peter Lake, *Moderate Puritans and the Elizabethan Church* (Cambridge, England: Cambridge University Press, 1982), 98–106, 166–67.

considering the Reformed background of Sibbes' preaching on the assurance of salvation.

Robert Middlekauf wrote that "the most familiar figure among Puritans is the tormented soul, constantly examining his every thought and action, now convinced that hell awaits him, now lunging after the straw of hope that he is saved, and then once more falling into despair. He wants to believe, he tries, he fails, he succeeds, he fails—always on the cycle of alternating moods."[6] John Calvin complained that this was exactly the "assurance mingled with doubt" that some were teaching in his own day:

> Whenever we look upon Christ, they confess that we find full occasion for good hope in him. But because we are always unworthy of all those benefits which are offered to us in Christ, they would have us waver and hesitate at the sight of our unworthiness. . . . Thus, when Satan once sees that those open devices with which he formerly had been wont to destroy the certainty of faith are now of no avail, he tries to sap it by covert devices.[7]

Was this teaching of an uncertain, wavering assurance that of Calvin's Reformed heirs, and particularly of Richard Sibbes?

---

6   Robert Middlekauff, "Piety and Intellect in Puritanism," *The William and Mary Quarterly*, 3rd series, vol. XXII/3 (July 1965): 459.

7   Calvin, *Institutes*, 3.2.24.

The post-Reformation Reformed understanding of assurance was a reaction against the Roman Catholic doctrine of assurance of salvation, which was codified at the Council of Trent in 1547.[8] The council defined justification as occurring over a period of time rather than a moment, saying that the Christian's initial justification—which occurs in baptism—can be lost through mortal sin.[9] Final justification, where sinners are judged by God as being righteous in His sight, necessarily follows sanctification because God cannot justify (pronounce righteous) sinners while they are still sinners.[10] Normally, the righteousness of Christ has to be imparted to them and grown throughout their lives by God's grace, administered through the seven sacraments of the church.

The Council of Trent's "Decree on Justification" states in chapter 9 what logically follows from such an understanding of justification, i.e., that "no one can know with a certitude of faith which cannot be subject to error, that he has obtained God's grace." Chapter 12 was directed explicitly against those who thought that they could definitely know they were among the elect, apart from special revelation.[11] To propagate a teaching of assurance of final justification, then, was taken as teaching sinners to think themselves perfect, a damning error.[12]

---

8 "Decree on Justification," repr. in *The Christian Faith in the Doctrinal Documents of the Catholic Church*, rev. ed., eds. J. Neuner and J. Dupuis (New York: Alba House, 1982), 554–70.

9 "Decree on Justification," chapter 15.

10 "Decree on Justification," chapter 14.

11 So also "Decree on Justification," canon 16.

12 "Decree on Justification," chapter 13, contains the "doctrine of doubt."

JOHN CALVIN

John Calvin wrote of salvation as if it included assurance,[13] and yet he also conceded that "we cannot imagine any certainty that is not tinged with doubt."[14] This was not to suggest the Roman position, "that faith does not rest in a certain and clear knowledge, but only in an obscure and confused knowledge of the divine will toward us,"[15] because "even if we are distracted by various thoughts, we are not on that account completely divorced from faith. . . . We see him [God] afar off, but so clearly as to know that we are not at all deceived."[16] Instead of experiencing lack of assurance from putting one's faith in an unsure source of salvation, Calvin said believers should "deeply fix all our hope [on God's promise], paying no regard to our works, to seek any help from them" in regards to the basis of salvation. This was not to say that the believer should disregard works when considering whether one has this salvation established on the basis of Christ's righteousness alone.[17] Assurance, in this sense—having a certain basis of salvation—is inherent in true faith.

---

13 E.g., his comments on Galatians 4:6 in his *Commentaries on the Epistles of Paul to the Galatians and Ephesians*, trans. William Pringle (Edinburgh, Scotland: 1854), 121 (yet it should be noted that Calvin makes this comment in the context of anti-Roman polemics); Calvin, *Institutes*, 3.2.7.

14 Calvin, *Institutes*, 3.2.16, 17. Cf. 3.2.18, 37; 3.13.3; 3.24.6.

15 Calvin, *Institutes*, 3.2.18.

16 Calvin, *Institutes*, 3.2.18–19; cf. 3.2.14.

17 Calvin, *Institutes*, 3.13.4; cf. 3.14.18; Lynn Baird Tipson Jr., "The Development of a Puritan Understanding of Conversion," (Ph.D. diss., Yale University: 1972),

Calvin taught that while it was theologically necessary to distinguish between justification and sanctification, they are never separable in the true believer's experience.[18] This inseparability of justification from sanctification in Calvin helps explain a certain amount of confusion regarding Calvin's position on assurance. Calvin has often been taken as affirming that saving faith necessarily includes assurance, with the implication being that the two are almost identical.[19] Yet many statements of Calvin show the fallacy of this conclusion.[20] While Calvin can be read as including assurance in initial, saving faith only by controverting other statements of his, he may more satisfactorily be read as affirming assurance as part of the Christian's normal, lifelong experience of saving faith. Thus, and only thus, does assurance become an experience of all Christians—though not at all times—gratuitous, yet clearly related to sanctification.

In 1539, Calvin prayed to God, remembering the situation before the Reformation—a situation in which "that confident hope of salvation, which is both enjoined by thy Word and founded upon it, had almost vanished. Indeed it

---

102–4, concluding that "Calvin very cautiously accepted the confirmatory evidence of good works while insisting that true faith was its own assurance."

18 Calvin, *Institutes*, 3.24.1.

19 This posited identification in Calvin, and their obvious separation in later Reformed thought, has, along with the related issue of covenant, been the moving force behind the idea that Calvin's heirs in England in the century following his death radically altered his theology (e.g., George Fisher, *History of Christian Doctrine* [Edinburgh, Scotland: 1896], 274, 299).

20 In Calvin, *Institutes*, 3.13.5.

was received as a kind of oracle; it was foolish arrogance, and, as they said, presumption, for any one to trust in thy goodness and the righteousness of thy Son, and entertain a sure and unfaltering hope of salvation."[21] In Calvin's teaching and preaching, the sudden acquisition of certain salvation would have been the experience of his previously Roman Catholic hearers as they came into the Protestant evangelical gospel, being taught for the first time that their justification was not dependent upon their sanctification, and that assurance was more available than most had imagined. The simple perseverance in abstaining from Roman practices and attending Protestant worship became an act and evidence of true faith. With such polemic dominating Calvin's understanding of faith, it is only natural that he should stress the primacy of the work of Christ.[22]

Even among those inwardly embracing the promises of God,[23] Calvin clearly spoke of "degrees of assurance" saying that they were "well known in the faith."[24] Calvin encouraged his hearers, in order to get this "assurance of the kingdom of

---

21 John Calvin, "Reply to Sadoleto" (1539), trans. J.K.S. Reid, *Calvin: Theological Treatises* (London: Westminster John Knox, 1954), 247. "The *Institutio* was addressed to men suffering under the pastoral cruelty of the mediaeval church" (T.H.L. Parker, *John Calvin: A Biography* (London: Westminster John Knox, 1975), 36).

22 Francois Wendel, *Calvin: Origins and Development of His Religious Thought*, trans. Philip Mariet (London: Collins, 1963), 262.

23 Calvin, *Institutes*, 3.2.16; cf. 3.24.4.

24 John Calvin, *Sermons on 2 Samuel*, trans. Douglas Kelly (Edinburgh, Scotland: Banner of Truth 1992), 199–201; cf. John Calvin, "Catechism of the Church of Geneva" (1545), trans. Reid, 104.

heaven," to look to the "pledge" that God had given believers "in the death and passion of our Lorde Jesus Christ."[25] "Christ . . . is the mirror wherein we must . . . contemplate our own election."[26] Yet Calvin also taught that, though any assurance of salvation based on one's own righteousness was impossible,[27] "we do not forbid him from undergirding and strengthening this faith by signs of the divine benevolence toward him."[28] Believers should consider "experience"[29] as a "confirmation of our fayth."[30] Though never saving, a righteous life was essential to "ratify"[31] the covenant God made with believers. Finally, realizing the problems of hypocrisy,[32] Calvin also stressed the need for the witness of the Holy Spirit as the "seale of our adoption,"[33] writing:

---

25 John Calvin, *The Sermons of M. John Calvin upon the Fifth Booke of Moses Called Deuteronomie*, trans. Arthur Golding (London: 1583), 28.b.40; cf. 913.a.10; Calvin, *Institutes*, 3.24.5.

26 Calvin, *Institutes*, 3.24.5; cf. 3.17.10; 3.16.1; Calvin, *Deuteronomie*, 532.a.10.

27 Cf. Calvin, *Institutes*, 3.17.5; cf. 3.13.3; 3.14.20.

28 Calvin, *Institutes*, 3.14.18; cf. 19–20; Calvin, *Galatians*, 121. William K.B. Stoever has maintained that this is the basis for the practical syllogism in Calvin (Stoever, *'A Faire and Easie Way to Heaven': Covenant Theology and Antinomianism in Early Massachusetts* [Middletown, Conn.: Wesleyan, 1978], 223n16).

29 Calvin, 2 *Samuel*, 201.

30 Calvin, *Deuteronomie*, 240.b.10; Calvin, *Institutes*, 3.8.1; Cf. Calvin, *A Commentary on the Harmony of the Gospels*, trans. T.H.L. Parker (Edinburgh, Scotland: Saint Andrews, 1972), II.194.

31 Calvin, *Deuteronomie*, 316.b.50; cf. 326.b.50; 554.b.50; 915.b.30-60; *Institutes*, 3.6.1; 3.16.1; John Calvin, *Commentaries on the Catholic Epistles*, trans. John Owen (Edinburgh, Scotland: 1855), 376–78.

32 Calvin, *Institutes*, 3.17.5.

33 Calvin, *Deuteronomie*, 913.b.60; cf. 316.b.50-317.a.10, 915.a.60; Calvin, *Galatians*, 121; Calvin, *Institutes*, 3.2.24.

Every one of us must have an eie to himself, so as the
gospel be not preached in vain nor we beare the bare
name of Christians, without shewing the effect of it
in our deedes. For until our adoption be sealed by the
holy Ghost, let us not thinke that it availeth us any
whit to have herd the word of God. . . . But when we
have once a warrant in our hearts, that his promises
belong unto us, & are behighted unto us, by reason
that we receive them with true obedience, & sticke to
our Lord Jesus Christ, suffering him to governe us:
that is a sure seale of God's chosing of us, so as we not
onely have the outwarde apparance of it before men,
but also the truth of it before our God.[34]

Calvin taught that subjective assurance was distinct from
saving faith, and came not through reflecting on one's own
belief but through looking to Christ as the sole basis of salvation, leading a Christian life and acknowledging the direct
witness of the Holy Spirit in the believer's heart.[35]

---

34 Calvin, *Deuteronomie*, 440.a.30.

35 Breward mistakenly portrayed Calvin as only presenting looking to Christ (though
    through church, Word and sacraments) as the avenue of assurance (Breward, 45).
    Therefore, the later prominence of assurance among the Puritans, Breward por-
    trayed as having come from Perkins.

THE ENGLISH REFORMERS
AND SIBBES' CONTEMPORARIES

William Tyndale,[36] Thomas Becon,[37] John Jewel,[38] and William Fulke[39] all presented this same tripartite basis of assurance, which was typical of the English Reformers' presentation; that is, assurance was seen to arise from the consideration of the objective work of Christ, the inner testimony of the Spirit, and the answering works of the regenerated life. In most of the writings of the English Reformers, the doctrine of assurance had been important primarily in anti-Roman apologetics. Bradford's writings are typical in that, as in Calvin, faith and assurance seem to be at points identified[40] and at other points distinguished.[41] Yet in his public utterances, Bradford seemed to unite both senses of assurance polemically, in order

---

36 William Tyndale, *Parable of the Wicked Mammon*, repr. in *Doctrinal Treatises*, ed. Henry Walter (Cambridge, England: 1848), 89 [Christ], 101; cf. 113; Tyndale, *Exposition of the First Epistle of St. John* (1531), reprinted in *Expositions and Notes*, ed. Henry Walter (Cambridge, England: 1849), 186, 207 [Spirit and Works].

37 Thomas Becon, "The Sick Man's Salve" in *Prayers and Other Pieces of Thomas Becon*, ed. John Ayre (Cambridge, England: 1844), 174, 176–78. Cf. Becon, "The Actes of Christe and Antichrist," in *Prayers*, 531.

38 In John Jewel, *A Defense of the Apologie of the Church of England, Conteining an Answer to a certaine Booke lately set forth by M. Harding*, in *The Works of John Jewel*, ed. John Ayre (Cambridge, England: 1848), 3:241, 245, 247.

39 William Fulke, *A Discoverie of the Daungerous Rocke of the Popish Church*, in *Stapleton's Fortress Overthrown . . .* , ed. Richard Gibbings (Cambridge, England: 1848), 229.

40 E.g., "Sermon on Repentance" in *The Writings of John Bradford*, ed. Aubrey Townsend (Cambridge, England: 1848) 76–77; "Fear," in *Writings*, 344.

41 E.g., "Meditations," prefixed to Tyndale's New Testament, in *Writings*, 252; letter to Robert Harrington and his wife, in *Writings*, 116–17; letter to Mary Honywood, in *Writings*, 132; cf. 151–56.

to clear the field of a Roman understanding of the gospel. In his private writings, he distinguished pastorally between assurance of Christ's sufficiency alone, and assurance of one's own apprehension of that. The distinction seemed to be clarified as the church's pastoral experience of doubt in the midst of an assured gospel grew. Thus, while the English Roman Catholic Gregory Martin's assumption that his Protestant opponents saw assurance as inextricably bound up with faith was not entirely unfounded, William Fulke could respond that assurance is certainly desirable, yet not necessary to salvation.[42]

William Perkins taught that assurance is the supreme case of conscience.[43] Though believers differ in degrees of assurance, he suggested that one could be sure, by examining oneself to see if one's faith did "purifie thy heart, and cleanse thy life, and cause thee to abound in good workes."[44] Not that Perkins suggested that good works can save a person; they merely witness to the reality of saving faith[45]—because election, vocation, faith, adoption, justification, sanctification, and glorification, though partially sequential, "are never separated in the salvation of any man, but like inseparable companions, goe hand

---

42 William Fulke, *A Defense of the sincere and true Translations of the holie Scriptures into the English tong* (Cambridge, England: 1843), 415.

43 William Perkins, *The Whole Treatise of the Cases of Conscience* (Cambridge, England: 1606), 73–87.

44 William Perkins, *A Clowd of Faithful Witnesses, Leading to the heavenly Canaan: Or, A Commentarie upon the 11. Chapter to the Hebrewes, preached in Cambridge* (n.l., 1609), 26.

45 William Perkins, *A Commentarie, or, Exposition Upon the five first Chapters of the Epistle to the Galatians* (Cambridge, England: 1617), 186, 502.

in hand."[46] Evidence of any one of them could serve as well for the others.

Furthermore, Perkins set forth the internal witness of the Spirit[47] (which comes usually "by the preaching, reading, and meditation of the word of God; as also by praier, and the right use of the Sacraments," and by the "effects and fruits of the Spirit"[48]) and the witness of the believer's sanctified spirit, or conscience (evidenced by grief for sin, resolution to repent, "savouring" the things of the Spirit, and appropriate works) as the two testimonies of adoption. Even if the fruit were small, Perkins encouraged his hearers to believe. He believed it was like:

> The man that is in close prison, if he sees but one little beame of the Sunne, by a small crevisse; by that very beame he hath use of the Sunne, though he seeth not the whole body of the Sunne. In like manner, though our faith, the hand of our soule, be mingled with weakness and corruption; though we feele never so little measure of God's grace in us; yea though our knowledge be never so small; yet it is an argument, that the Spirit of God beginnes to worke in our harts, and that we have by Gods mercie, begunne to lay hold on Christ.[49]

---

46 Perkins, *Cases*, 74. So too, Calvin, *Institutes*, 3.16.1.
47 Cf. William Perkins, "The Foundation of Christian Religion Gathered into Six Principles," reprinted in Breward, 155–56, 158.
48 Perkins, *Cases*, 76.
49 Perkins, *Cases*, 347 (cf. 78).

Perkins exhorted his doubting hearers to "beginne with faith, and in the first place, simply beleeve Gods promises; and afterward we come, by the goodnes of God, to feele and have experience of his mercie."[50]

Reformed confessional statements[51] from the period largely presented assurance in the same way, affirming each of the tripartite bases outlined above. So too did Sibbes' contemporaries. In many ways, the Westminster Assembly's teaching acts as a summary to the Reformed doctrine of assurance in the previous century. Instructed by long experience of anti-Roman polemics and pastoral ministry, the assembly produced a balanced statement protecting against hypocrisy on one hand and an uncritical identification of saving faith with assurance on the other.

Chapter 20, which deals with assurance, contains four articles. In the first, the possibility of assurance is set forth, clearly distinguished from the vain deceits of hypocrites. In the second, the foundation of this assurance is said to be the "divine truth of the promises of salvation" and the inward evidence of "the testimony of the Spirit of adoption witnessing with our spirits that we are the children of God." In the third, assurance is distinguished from the "essence of faith," and yet,

---

50 Perkins, *Cases*, 347.

51 "The Lambeth Articles" in Philip Schaff, ed., *The Creeds of Christendom with a History and Critical Notes*, 6th ed. (New York: 1931), 3:524; cf. H.G. Porter, *Reformation and Reaction in Tudor Cambridge* (Cambridge, England: 1958), 335–36, 365–71); "The Irish Articles of Religion," in Schaff, 3:534; Fifth Head, Article V, "Canons of the Synod of Dort" in Schaff, 3:593.

since it was attainable, "it is the duty of everyone to give all diligence to make his calling and election sure; that thereby his heart may be enlarged in peace and joy in the Holy Ghost, in love and thankfulness to God, and in strength and cheerfulness in the duties of obedience, the proper fruits of assurance: so far is it from inclining men to looseness." In the final article, the shaking, diminishing, and intermitting of assurance in the experience of believers is clearly allowed.

EVIDENCE OF ASSURANCE

Sibbes took it as axiomatic that Christians could and should be assured of their faith, given the gospel he espoused.[52] This persuasion of God's love involves a "double act of faith."[53] First there is "an act whereby the soul relies upon God as reconciled in Christ, and relies upon Christ as given of God, and relies upon the promise."[54] This is the gift of saving faith every Christian has. Also, "there is a reflect act, wherby, knowing we do thus, we have assurance." Yet this second act is not always done by all Christians: "We first by faith apply ourselves to God, and then apply God to us, to be ours; the first is the conflicting exercise of faith, the last is the triumph of faith;

---

52 "First Chapter 2 Corinthians," in *Works*, 3:466; cf. "Bowels Opened," in *Works*, in *Works*, 2:47.

53 "First Chapter 2 Corinthians," in *Works*, 3:467; cf. "Yea and Amen," in *Works*, 4:142; "Salvation Applied," in *Works*, 5:393; "Faith Triumphant," in *Works*, 7:430.

54 "First Chapter 2 Corinthians," in *Works*, 3:467.

therefore faith properly is not assurance."[55] Saving faith and assurance are not to be confused (as the Roman Catholics had taken the Protestants to do). "Some think they have no faith at all, because they have no full assurance" but they were mistaken.[56]

Furthermore, Sibbes admitted that there were "carnal men" who presumptuously "would have heaven, if they might have it with their lusts."[57] In the hour of trial, however, when needing true comfort, Sibbes said, their hypocrisy would be revealed by their lack of assurance.[58]

Sibbes taught that one did not get assurance through merit,[59] nor through considering election[60] or for whom particularly Christ died.[61] Fundamentally, "The Holy Ghost must ascertain this."[62] True, there was the assurance that was the simple reflection of the man's own spiritual understanding.[63] This was not, however, the work of the Spirit; the Spirit's special sealing would come in times of great temptation and trial

---

55 "Soul's Conflict," in *Works*, 1:266; cf. "Yea and Amen," in *Works*, 4:142.

56 "Bruised Reed," in *Works*, 1:62; cf. Von Rohr, 65–68.

57 "Salvation Applied," in *Works*, 5:391; cf. "Demand," in *Works*, 7:483; "First Chapter 2 Corinthians," in *Works*, 3:454, 458, 464, 469; "Bride's Longing," in *Works*, 6:545.

58 "First Chapter 2 Corinthians," in *Works*, 3:458.

59 "Excellency," in *Works*, 4:296–97.

60 "First Chapter 2 Corinthians," in *Works*, 3:156; "Glance of Heaven," in *Works*, 4:182; "Glimpse," in *Works*, 7:496; Calvin, *Institutes*, 3.21.1.

61 "Angels," in *Works*, 6:354; "Glance of Heaven," in *Works*, 4:182.

62 "Angels," in *Works*, 6:352; cf. "Excellency," in *Works*, 4:220, 296; "Description," in *Works*, 1:21–22; "Faithful Covenanter," in *Works*, 6:9; "Soul's Conflict," in *Works*, 1:269; "First Chapter 2 Corinthians," in *Works*, 3:455–56.

63 "First Chapter 2 Corinthians," in *Works*, 3:455–56.

when "the soul is so carried and hurried that it cannot reflect upon itself, nor know what is in itself without much ado."[64]

Nevertheless, even this seal had to be defined, which Sibbes did by noting four works of the Spirit in the soul: (1) His "secret voice . . . to the soul, that we are 'the sons of God'"; (2) His granting believers boldness to approach God; (3) sanctification; (4) peace of conscience and joy in the Holy Ghost.[65] The testimony of the Holy Spirit is answered in the believer's spirit by "evidences of grace stamped upon his heart."[66] Such heart-evidences include "discontent with our present ill estate,"[67] the simple belief in God as one is drawn to Him,[68] finding comfort in the promises of God,[69] familiarity with God and consequent boldness to approach Him as Father,[70] desires to be increasingly transformed like Christ,[71] comfortable thoughts of death,[72] and willingness to die for God's

---

64 "First Chapter 2 Corinthians," in *Works*, 3:456.

65 "First Chapter 2 Corinthians," in *Works*, 3:456; cf. "Soul's Conflict," in *Works*, 1:288–89.

66 "First Chapter 2 Corinthians," in *Works*, 3:445; cf. 454, 457; "Demand," in *Works*, 7:483; "Danger," in *Works*, 7:413; "Divine Meditations," in *Works*, 7:189, 223; "Glance of Heaven," in *Works*, 4:182; "Bruised Reed," in *Works*, 1:69; Preston, *Breast-Plate*, pt. ii, 84–85.

67 "Bowels Opened," in *Works*, 2:117; cf. "Bruised Reed," in *Works*, 1:97.

68 "First Chapter 2 Corinthians," in *Works*, 3:156; "Soul's Conflict," in *Works*, 1:198.

69 "First Chapter 2 Corinthians," in *Works*, 3:452; "Bowels Opened," in *Works*, 2:176.

70 "First Chapter 2 Corinthians," in *Works*, 3:456–57; cf. "Christian's Work," in *Works*, 5:25; "Faithful Covenanter," in *Works*, 6:12–13; "Knot of Prayer," in *Works*, 7:247; "Christ's Suffering," in *Works*, 1:364; "Excellency," in *Works*, 4:231–33; "Recommendation," Henry Scudder, *A Key of Heaven, The Lord's Prayer Opened* (London: 1620); repr. in *Works*, 1:lxxxvii–lxxxix.

71 "First Chapter 2 Corinthians," in *Works*, 3:453.

72 "First Chapter 2 Corinthians," in *Works*, 3:442; cf. "Yea and Amen," in *Works*, 4:131.

truth.[73] Even the desire for assurance, Sibbes said, is a ground of it.[74]

In times of unusual trial, an extraordinary seal of assurance is given—"the joy of the Holy Ghost and peace of conscience."[75] These are worked by the Spirit in the soul of the believer to give assurance, but neither is the universal experience of believers. Such extraordinary seals God gives, "even as parents, smile upon their children when they need it most."[76]

After discoursing on seals and hypocrisy, Sibbes turns to his hearers and, with an arresting change of expression to the second person, asks them, "Did you ever feel the joy of the Spirit in holy duties, after inward striving against your lusts, and getting ground of them? This is a certain sign that God hath sealed you."[77]

Sanctification, too, Sibbes presented as an evidence of salvation.[78] In a sense, every description of a Christian by Sibbes in a sermon was an invitation to his hearers to evaluate themselves, to find bases of similarity and thus hope, or difference and thus conviction.[79] He wrote: "When two masters

---

73 "Danger," in *Works*, 7:411; "Soul's Conflict," in *Works*, 1:252.

74 "Spouse," in *Works*, 2:204.

75 "First Chapter 2 Corinthians," in *Works*, 3:457; cf. 458–59; "Soul's Conflict," in *Works*, 1:288–89.

76 "First Chapter 2 Corinthians," in *Works*, 3:458.

77 "Yea and Amen," in *Works*, 4:136; cf. "First Chapter 2 Corinthians," in *Works*, 3:458; "Description," in *Works*, 1:22; "Excellency," in *Works*, 4:222.

78 "Returning Backslider," in *Works*, 2:255–56.

79 E.g., "First Chapter 2 Corinthians," in *Works*, 3:447; "Rich Poverty," in *Works*, 6:257; "Difficulty," in *Works*, 1:396.

are parted, their servants will be known whom they serve, by following their own master. Blessed be God, in these times we enjoy both religion and the world together; but if times of suffering should approach, then it would be known whose servants we are. . . . If trouble and persecution should arise, wouldst thou stand up for Christ, and set light by liberty, riches, credit, all in comparison of him?"[80]

Though he was certain that works of themselves are worthless when considering justification, Sibbes pointed out that Paul "glories not in his conversation and sincerity as a title, but he glories in it as an evidence that his title is good."[81] In that sense, "we must all read our happiness in our holiness."[82] Yet the imperfection of sanctification, and particularly one's perception of one's own sanctification, make it uncertain evidence. Sibbes said that Christians "have so different judgments of themselves, looking sometimes at the work of grace, sometimes at the remainder of corruption, and when they look upon that, then they think they have no grace."[83]

Yet this was not the "half-papist" teaching that Calvin had lamented; the crucial difference was that Calvin's antagonists were teaching that the Christian should so doubt because of "the sight of our own unworthiness," whereas Sibbes taught

---

80 "Danger," in *Works*, 7:412; cf. "Faithful Covenanter," in *Works*, 6:14.

81 "First Chapter 2 Corinthians," in *Works*, 3:205.

82 "First Chapter 2 Corinthians," in *Works*, 3:469; cf. 446, 478; "Bruised Reed," in *Works*, 1:87; "Description," in *Works*, 1:14, 22; "Yea and Amen," in *Works*, 4:145; "Excellency," in *Works*, 4:221, 231; "Faithful Covenanter," in *Works*, 6:14.

83 "Bruised Reed," in *Works*, 1:50.

that the Christian *would* so doubt because of the "remainder of corruption." The former taught that one should look to Christ and oneself in order to be saved; the latter that one should look to Christ and oneself in order to see if one *had been* saved. Whatever similarities there may have been were outweighed by their differences. Sibbes taught that, however little in measure, if the sanctification in the believer's life was authentic, it could provide much comfort[84]: "A spark of fire is but little, yet it is fire as well as the whole element of fire; and a drop of water, it is water as well as the whole ocean. When a man is in a dark place . . . if he have a little light shining in to him from a little crevice, that little light discovers that the day is broke, that the sun is risen."[85]

Therefore, Sibbes encouraged believers to examine "rather the truth, than the measure of any grace."[86] Any opposition to sin was a meaningful sign of grace, "though we shall have much opposition, yet if we strive, he will help us; if we fail, he will cherish us; if we be guided by him, we shall overcome; if we overcome, we are sure to be crowned. . . . This very belief, that faith shall be victorious, is a means to make it so indeed."[87]

---

84 "First Chapter 2 Corinthians," in *Works*, 3:465, 470.
85 "First Chapter 2 Corinthians," in *Works*, 3:470–71; cf. "Bowels Opened," in *Works*, 2:117; "Bruised Reed," in *Works*, 1:99. The use of this example by Calvin, Perkins, and Sibbes shows up the fallacy in the substantial contrast Pettit has suggested between Sibbes and "most before him" (Pettit, *The Heart Prepared*, 70; cf. 73–74).
86 "First Chapter 2 Corinthians," in *Works*, 3:471.
87 "Bruised Reed," in *Works*, 1:99, 100.

THE ABUSE AND USE OF ASSURANCE

Sibbes realized that the awareness of salvation is not always present in the believer.[88] Whether through sin[89] or Satan,[90] divine desertions[91] or the believers' carelessness,[92] natural tempers or spiritual maturity,[93] many reasons can account for different experiences of assurance. Contrary to what he felt was the incalculably cruel pastoral doctrine of the uncertainty of salvation, Sibbes taught that it was the duty of each Christian to labor for the assurance of salvation.[94] To ignore the search for assurance was tantamount to ignoring the search for salvation—not because assurance was saving, but because it was assurance of the salvation one needed.[95]

Therefore, Sibbes stressed the need for assurance, its benefits, and its comforts in almost every sermon.[96] Christians

88 "First Chapter 2 Corinthians," in *Works*, 3:466–67.

89 "First Chapter 2 Corinthians," in *Works*, 3:478; cf. "Christ is Best," in *Works*, 1:346; "Divine Meditations," in *Works*, 7:211–12.

90 "Sword," in *Works*, 1:110.

91 "First Chapter 2 Corinthians," in *Works*, 3:482; "Faith Triumphant," in *Works*, 7:430–31.

92 "Church's Riches," in *Works*, 4:517; cf. "Two Sermons," in *Works*, 7:353; "Soul's Conflict," in *Works*, 1:199; "Faith Triumphant," in *Works*, 7:430.

93 "First Chapter 2 Corinthians," in *Works*, 3:467; cf. "Church's Riches," in *Works*, 4:510; "Faithful Covenanter," in *Works*, 6:21.

94 "First Chapter 2 Corinthians," in *Works*, 3:468; cf. 466, 476; "Description," in *Works*, 1:23; "Glimpse," in *Works*, 7:495; "Christ is Best," in *Works*, 1:342; "Two Sermons," in *Works*, 7:352; "Soul's Conflict," in *Works*, 1:124. Some of Sibbes' most regular and most heated anti-Roman rhetoric comes in discussions of this pastoral issue.

95 "Returning Backslider," in *Works*, 2:264.

96 E.g., "Church's Visitation," in *Works*, 1:381–82; "Danger," in *Works*, 7:411; "First Chapter 2 Corinthians," in *Works*, 3:460, 462, 466, 475; "Sword," in *Works*, 1:107;

are to labor to gain assurance in order "that God may have more honour, and that we may have more comfort from him again, and walk more cheerfully through the troubles and temptations that are in the world."[97] For how could believers be thankful, be joyful, willingly endure trials, if not assured of the outcome?"[98] To Sibbes, assurance seemed to grant the believer a kind of spiritual invulnerability[99]:

> Oh, what should water my heart, and make it melt in obedience unto my God, but the assurance and knowledge of the virtue of this most precious blood of my Redeemer, applied to my sick soul, in the full and free remission of all my sins, and appeasing the justice of God? . . . Down, then, with this false opinion and perverse doctrine, which overthroweth all the comfort of godliness, faith, and obedience to God.[100]

Finally, only an assured soul will find comfort at the hour of death, for "death, with the eternity of misery after it, who

---

Frank E. Farrell, "Richard Sibbes: A Study in Early Seventeenth Century English Puritanism" [Ph.D diss., University of Edinburgh: 1955], 221.

97 "First Chapter 2 Corinthians," in *Works*, 3:468.

98 "First Chapter 2 Corinthians," in *Works*, 3:483; cf. "Glimpse," in *Works*, 7:495; "Returning Backslider," in *Works*, 2:273; "Spouse," in *Works*, 2:206; "Saint's Safety," in *Works*, 1:330–31; "Fourth Chapter 2 Corinthians," in *Works*, 4:450.

99 "Spouse," in *Works*, 2:207; "First Chapter 2 Corinthians," in *Works*, 3:91–93; "Art," in *Works*, 5:193; "God's Inquisition," in *Works*, 6:213.

100 "Glimpse," in *Works*, 7:495; cf. "Christ is Best," in *Works*, 1:341; "Returning Backslider," in *Works*, 2:264.

can look it in the face, without hope of life everlasting, without assurance of a happy change after death?"[101]

GAINING ASSURANCE

To grow assurance, one should "attend upon the ordinances of God, and use all kinds of spiritual means."[102] This includes attending preaching of the Word, meditating on it, reading the Bible and other good books, keeping good company, and taking care not to grieve the Holy Spirit.[103] The conscience must be heeded,[104] and the Word heard must be obeyed.[105]

To those attempting to regain assurance after sin—"wilful breeches in sanctification"—Sibbes taught that "such must give a sharp sentence against themselves, and yet cast themselves upon God's mercy in Christ, as at their first conversion."[106] In situations where one is not sure of the reason for a lack of assurance, Sibbes taught that one first looks for those extraordinary and obvious signs; joy in the Holy Ghost and peace of conscience.[107] Yet, the Christian knows that when he "finds

101 "First Chapter 2 Corinthians," in *Works*, 3:483; cf. 460, 464; "Bride's Longing," in *Works*, 6:552; "Christ is Best," in *Works*, 1:342.

102 "First Chapter 2 Corinthians," in *Works*, 3:480; "Divine Meditations," in *Works*, 7:209.

103 "First Chapter 2 Corinthians," in *Works*, 3:480–81; cf. Nuttall, *Holy Spirit*, 23–24.

104 "Demand," in *Works*, 7:486.

105 "Witness," in *Works*, 7:383; cf. "Excellency," in *Works*, 4:296–97; "Faith Triumphant," in *Works*, 7:432, 436–37; "Bowels Opened," in *Works*, 2:26; "Angels," in *Works*, 6:354.

106 "Bruised Reed," in *Works*, 1:70; cf. "Soul's Conflict," in *Works*, 1:123–24, 234.

107 "First Chapter 2 Corinthians," in *Works*, 3:459; cf. "Glimpse," in *Works*, 7:496.

not extraordinary comfort from God's Spirit, that God's love is constant;" he can, therefore, reason from God's past love to his present love.[108]

The believer should be encouraged by the work of sanctification in life, however small. "Be not discouraged, when the stamp in wax is almost out, it is current in law. Put the case the stamp of the prince be an old coin (as sometimes we see it on a king Harry groat), yet it is current money, yea, though it be a little cracked."[109] Still other times, friends "can read our evidences better than ourselves."[110]

Nevertheless Sibbes was intent on not minimizing the gratuitous nature of Christian salvation. When comfort was wanting, "we must judge ourselves . . . by faith, and not by feeling; looking to the promises and word of God, and not to our present sense and apprehension."[111] Like Calvin, Sibbes taught that even the best actions of the believer "need Christ to perfume them";[112] relying too much on works is always a danger in the human heart. "Another cause of disquiet is, that men by a natural kind of popery seek for their comfort too much sanctification, neglecting justification, relying too

---

108 "First Chapter 2 Corinthians," in *Works*, 3:459.
109 "First Chapter 2 Corinthians," in *Works*, 3:461; cf. the list of eleven evidences on 472–75; cf. lists in the following: "Bowels Opened," in *Works*, 2:148, 154–55; "Bruised Reed," in *Works*, 1:87; "Returning Backslider," in *Works*, 2:255–56; "Rich Poverty," in *Works*, 6:254–63; "Witness," in *Works*, 7:380; Nuttall, *Holy Spirit*, 59.
110 "Bowels Opened," in *Works*, 2:107; cf. 131; "Soul's Conflict," in *Works*, 1:194.
111 "Bowels Opened," in *Works*, 2:103.
112 "Bruised Reed," in *Works*, 1:50.

much upon their own performances."[113] When corruption is so strong that one can see nothing of sanctification, the believer should remember that one's salvation did not come from assurance and that

> God can see somewhat of his own Spirit in that confusion, but the spirit [of the believer] itself cannot. Then go to the blood of Christ! There is always comfort. . . . before we go to Christ it is sufficient that we see nothing in ourselves, no qualification; for the graces of the Spirit they are not the condition of coming to Christ, but the promise of those that receive Christ after. Therefore go to Christ when thou feelest neither joy of the Spirit, nor sanctification of the Spirit . . . and that will purge thee, and wash thee from all thy sins.[114]

Though "the evidence indeed to prove our faith to be a true faith, is from works, . . . the title we have is only by Christ, only by grace."[115] This was to be the ultimate basis of assurance for the Christian, because "We are more safe in his comprehending of us, than in our clasping and holding of

---

113 "Soul's Conflict," in *Works*, 1:138.

114 "First Chapter 2 Corinthians," in *Works*, 3:464; cf. 476–77; "Bowels Opened," in *Works*, 2:157; "Divine Meditations," in *Works*, 7:211; "Soul's Conflict," in *Works*, 1:124, 212–13; "Witness," in *Works*, 7:378.

115 "Faithful Covenanter," in *Works*, 6:5.

him. As we say of the mother and the child, both hold, but the safety of the child is that the mother holds him."[116]

In summary, Sibbes presented assurance as a secondary act of faith, not given to all Christians, but available depending upon the will of God and the actions of the believer.[117] Since it is possible for true Christians to doubt their salvation and hypocrites to delude themselves, assurance of salvation is necessarily to be sought. Theologically, the assurance sought by Sibbes was typical of Protestants; it was not a prediction so much as a diagnosis. The matter that was uncertain in Sibbes' discussions of assurance was not salvation itself, but rather the perception of it. While Sibbes and others did teach (as had their Reformed predecessors, including Calvin) that "good works" are confirming of salvation, they did not teach that such works are either present or obvious at all times to the elect, or that they are present only in the elect. Sibbes affirmed what might well be called the Reformed tripartite basis of assurance: the consideration of the objective work of Christ, the inner testimony of the Spirit, and the answering works of the regenerated life.[118]

Consistent with his pastoral setting, Sibbes particularly focused on the continuing reality of doubt in the believer's life. This element is more prominent in pastoral writings than in

---

116 "Bowels Opened," in *Works*, 2:184.

117 See Stoever, 129–37.

118 Cf. Heinrich Heppe, *Reformed Dogmatics Set Out and Illustrated from the Sources*, trans. G.T. Thomson (London: 1950), 585–89.

polemical writings. The life of the believer is always evidence of his spiritual state, but not always discernable; at times of particular need, the Spirit witnesses internally to the troubled believer. Yet, throughout his preaching, Sibbes was clear that the objective work of Christ is the sole basis not merely of salvation in abstraction, but of one's own participation in it. For the certainty of this, he taught that the conscience played a pivotal role.

CHAPTER SEVEN

The Role
of Conscience

The natural faculties are not all that compose a person; God has, "in great mercy," left the conscience.[1] Sibbes taught that the conscience in man acts as God's "vicar; a little god in us to do his office, to call upon us, direct us, check and condemn us."[2] This quotation summarizes the different roles of the conscience in conviction and conversion, in sanctification and guidance.

Throughout his sermons, Sibbes spoke of the conscience in exalted terms, as God's "vicegerent and deputy in us,"[3] God's judge, His throne in the soul, His "hall, as it were, wherein he keeps his first judgment, wherein he keeps his assizes."[4] To his

---

1   "First Chapter 2 Corinthians," in *Works*, 3:209.

2   "Bowels Opened," in *Works*, 2:62; cf. "St. Paul's Challenge," in *Works*, in *Works*, 7:395; "Demand," in *Works*, 7:486; "Soul's Conflict," in *Works*, 1:148, 211.

3   "Judgment," in *Works*, 4:83; "First Chapter 2 Corinthians," in *Works*, 3:209.

4   "Bowels Opened," in *Works*, 2:107–8; "Bruised Reed," in *Works*, 1:78, 84; "First

lawyer listeners at Gray's Inn, he expanded Pauline legal imagery of the conscience, speaking of it as the informer, accuser, witness, judge, and executioner,[5] together in the under court of God's justice, the lower "court of conscience."[6] The conscience is essentially "to take God's part" in us.[7] It is a "chaplain in ordinary, a domestical divine" within the soul.[8] Drawing from Greek and Latin etymologies, Sibbes taught that conscience is a special universal "knowledge together with God," especially a "knowledge of the heart with God" put in the soul by God.[9] Even the illiterate can "read" this "book,"[10] which is "written in their hearts."[11]

THE INNER WITNESS

Sibbes taught that the primary way the conscience takes God's part in the soul is "to witness against us for our sins,"

Chapter 2 Corinthians," in *Works*, 3:211.

5 "First Chapter 2 Corinthians," in *Works*, 3:210; "Soul's Conflict," in *Works*, 1:144–45; Cf. "Bowels Opened," in *Works*, 2:94.

6 "Judgment," in *Works*, 4:85, 91–92; "Soul's Conflict," in *Works*, 1:144–45; "First Chapter 2 Corinthians," in *Works*, 3:210. Cf. Calvin, *Institutes*, 3.13.3; 3.19.15; 4.10.3.

7 "Soul's Conflict," in *Works*, 1:175; cf. "Fountain Sealed," in *Works*, 5:419.

8 "First Chapter 2 Corinthians," in *Works*, 3:212.

9 "Yea and Amen," in *Works*, 4:118; "First Chapter 2 Corinthians," in *Works*, 3:208–10; Calvin, *Institutes*, 3.19.15; cf. 4.10.3); Gouge, pt. xiii, 155 (Gouge's treatment of the conscience in this section is a model of the Ramist practise of understanding by division).

10 "Demand," in *Works*, 7:489–90.

11 "First Chapter 2 Corinthians," in *Works*, 3:210.

(reflecting Rom. 2:15).[12] Those who live in sins against conscience abuse their Christian liberty,[13] weaken their faith[14] and affection to goodness, and decay their love to God and sense of God's favor.[15] They are stopped from going boldly to God, because they stop the mouth of their conscience.[16] Such people Sibbes described as "dead to good actions"[17] and "worse than Sodomites."[18] They renounce their baptism, feed their corruptions,[19] deaden their spirits[20] and waste their comfort.[21] Furthermore, they give evidence that Christ is not teaching them by His Spirit.[22] They must not think that they love God,[23] that His Spirit is in them, that they have anything to do with Christ, that God is merciful,[24] or that they will go to heaven.[25] Though they are under the livery of Christ,

---

12 "Bowels Opened," in *Works*, 2:111; cf. "Angels," in *Works*, 6:333; "Christ's Suffering," in *Works*, 1:360; "Art," in *Works*, 5:183; John Calvin, *Commentary on Romans*, trans. R. Mackenzie (Edinburgh, Scotland: 1960), 49; Calvin, *Institutes*, 3.19.15; 4.10.3; Heinrich Bullinger, too, in his *Decades* (Cambridge, England: 1849), 1:194–95.

13 "Divine Meditations," in *Works*, 7:194.

14 "Excellency," in *Works*, 4:254; "Knot of Prayer," in *Works*, 7:242.

15 "Privileges," in *Works*, 5:283.

16 "Demand," in *Works*, 7:488; "Excellency," in *Works*, 4:254; "Knot of Prayer," in *Works*, 7:242.

17 "Excellency," in *Works*, 4:237.

18 "Ungodly's Misery," in *Works*, 1:389.

19 "Demand," in *Works*, 7:487.

20 "Knot of Prayer," in *Works*, 7:242.

21 "Divine Meditations," in *Works*, 7:194.

22 "Description," in *Works*, 1:23.

23 "Privileges," in *Works*, 5:281.

24 "Description," in *Works*, 1:23.

25 "Divine Meditations," in *Works*, 7:189; "Saint's Safety," in *Works*, 1:328.

they serve the enemy of Christ,[26] and therefore can look for nothing but vengeance from God.[27] Such "a galled conscience cannot endure God's presence"[28] because it gives us only fear and terror, especially of God.[29]

Instead of being disregarded, the conviction of conscience is to be heeded. Sibbes taught that there are two kinds of conviction by the conscience: natural and spiritual.[30] The first, common conviction of conscience, is weak; it does not change a man, but merely torments him.[31] All non-Christians experience this natural conviction of the Spirit.[32] With pathetic imagery, Sibbes described this fear of conscience in the unregenerate man: he "cannot go home to his own conscience"[33] because he is afraid of his own conscience; the unregenerate are "strangers at home, afraid of nothing more than themselves."[34] Sibbes illustrated the tortures of a guilty conscience by the example of Charles IX "who at night, when conscience hath the fittest time to work, a man being retired, then he

---

26 "Angels," in *Works*, 6:343; "Demand," in *Works*, 7:487.

27 "Demand," in *Works*, 7:490–91.

28 "Breathing," in *Works*, 2:223.

29 "Soul's Conflict," in *Works*, 1:222; "Rich Poverty," in *Works*, 6:261.

30 "Divine Meditations," in *Works*, 7:210.

31 "Soul's Conflict," in *Works*, 1:152; cf. "First Chapter 2 Corinthians," in *Works*, 3:90–91, 209; "Saint's Safety," in *Works*, 1:298–99; Calvin, *Institutes*, 3.13.3.

32 "First Chapter 2 Corinthians," in *Works*, 3:222, 208; cf. "Excellency," in *Works*, 4:278; "Angels," in *Works*, 6:348; "Soul's Conflict," in *Works*, 1:153; Calvin, *Institutes*, 4.20.16; Calvin, *Romans*, 37, 48.

33 "Saint's Hiding-Place," in *Works*, 1:406.

34 "Soul's Conflict," in *Works*, 1:145, 228; cf. "First Chapter 2 Corinthians," in *Works*, 3:224.

would have his singing boys, after he had betrayed them in that horrible massacre, after which he never had peace and quiet."[35]

One of Sibbes' most often repeated ideas is that the conscience will inevitably fulfill its role as judge, in this life or the next[36]: "The more their conscience is silenced and violenced in this world, the more vocal it shall be at the hour of death, and the day of judgment."[37] Therefore Sibbes encouraged his hearers to give heed to their consciences now, since God may make their bed their grave.[38] They should befriend their conscience presently, because "conscience . . . is either the greatest friends or the greatest enemy in the world."[39]

Aided and enlightened by the Spirit, the conscience prevails upon a man to follow his conscience fully and to take God's part against himself.[40] God's intention in planting the accusing conscience in man was always to triumph over it by

35 "First Chapter 2 Corinthians," in *Works*, 3:226.
36 "Bowels Opened," in *Works*, 2:111; "Bruised Reed," in *Works*, 1:97; "Christ is Best," in *Works*, 1:342; "Excellency," in *Works*, 4:254; "Soul's Conflict," in *Works*, 1:150; "First Chapter 2 Corinthians," in *Works*, 3:211. Cf. Bullinger, 1:195–96.
37 "First Chapter 2 Corinthians," in *Works*, 3:226; cf. 212, 224; "Fountain Opened," in *Works*, 5:494–95; "Angels," in *Works*, 6:345; "Christ is Best," in *Works*, 1:342; " Saint's Comforts," in *Works*, 6:172; "Excellency," in *Works*, 4:276; "Yea and Amen," in *Works*, 4:140; "Inquisition," in *Works*, 6:17; "Christ's Suffering," in *Works*, 1:363; Calvin, *Institutes*, 3.12.4; 4.10.3.
38 "Judgment," in *Works*, 4:85, 91–92; "Soul's Conflict," in *Works*, 1:144–45; "First Chapter 2 Corithians," in *Works*, 3:224, 226.
39 "Demand," in *Works*, 7:490; "First Chapter 2 Corinthians," in *Works*, 3:224; "Christ's Suffering," in *Works*, 1:363; "Judgment," in *Works*, 4:91; "Saint's Hiding-Place," in *Works*, 1:146; cf. Calvin, *Romans*, 49.
40 "Divine Meditations," in *Works*, 7:210.

Christ[41] who, by His Spirit, takes and purges the conscience, washing it in His own blood and thereby finally pacifying it.[42]

CONVICTION AND SANCTIFICATION

In what may seem unusual today, Sibbes presented faith not as presupposing personal security, but as rather fundamentally antithetical to it and as always guarding against it. He taught that "security" is a dangerous state, because in it the believer ceases attending to conscience.[43] A security that can dispense with conscience is not for this world; instead, the conscience has a role not merely in conversion, but also in sanctification, requiring the Christian's attention to his conscience.

Sibbes argued for this ongoing role for conscience for two reasons. The first reason is because conscience is important: "every man is to follow most what his own conscience, after information, dictates unto him; because conscience is God's deputy in us, and under God most to be regarded, and whosoever sins against it, in his own construction sins against God."[44] The second reason is that conscience is delicate and can be suppressed or warped.[45] He warned his hearers, "you have some that, for frowns of greatness, fear of loss, or for

---

41 "Fountain Opened," in *Works*, 5:482.
42 "Two Sermons," in *Works*, 7:345; cf. Calvin, *Institutes*, 3.13.3.
43 "Judgment," in *Works*, 4:90–92.
44 "Soul's Conflict," in *Works*, 1:211.
45 "Bruised Reed," in *Works*, 1:57.

hope of rising, will warp their conscience, and do anything."[46] Therefore, because of both its importance and its delicacy, the conscience was to be carefully examined.[47] A lack of peace in the conscience of a Christian most likely indicated some guilt that needed to be examined;[48] the "peace of conscience is above all good that can be desired."[49] Therefore, Sibbes advised a Separatist friend who was suffering from an afflicted conscience: "My earnest suit and desire is, that you would diligently peruse the booke of your conscience, enter into a thorow search and examination of your heart and life; and every day before you go to bed, take a time of recollection and meditation."[50] Instead of leading to petty spiritual bookkeeping, Sibbes suggested that such "a search into our own conscience and ways will force us to live by faith every day in Christ Jesus"[51] as we see the greatness of our need and of His provision.

Conscience and Assurance

If security is not for this world, what of assurance? Does attention to conscience entail a lack of assurance for the believer? Sibbes asked, "What good will it do to know in general that

46 "Bowels Opened," in *Works*, 2:158; cf. "Bruised Reed," in *Works*, 1:57–58; "Bowels Opened," in *Works*, 2:111.

47 "Bowels Opened," in *Works*, 2:50; cf. "Church's Riches," in *Works*, 4:517; "First Chapter 2 Corinthians," in *Works*, 3:222–23; Calvin, *Institutes*, 3.12.5.

48 "Soul's Conflict," in *Works*, 1:123–24.

49 "Providence," in *Works*, 5:54; "Christ Is Best," in *Works*, 1:342.

50 "Consolatory Letter," in *Works*, 1:cxiv; cf. "First Chapter 2 Corinthians," in *Works*, 3:226.

51 "Fountain Opened," in *Works*, 5:524.

Christ came to save sinners, and yet go to hell for all that?"[52] Sibbes taught that the believer can know his estate, and that it is the role of the conscience to try the claims of the believer to be in a state of grace.[53]

Two common problems when it comes to assurance for Christians are false guilt on one hand and false security on the other. Sibbes noted that sometimes errors of conscience are taken as its witness "when they regard rules which they should not, or when they mistake the matter and do not argue aright."[54] Thus, one is to reason with oneself, with the help of Scripture or friends who can see the error, whether the basis of a conscience that is peaceful before God is the blood of Christ rather than meritorious works.[55]

Then there is the problem of false security. Any peace that the conscience seems to give must reflect "grace working" in one's life, not simple carnal security. Christ "first . . . gives righteousness, and then he speaks peace to the conscience."[56] In this sense alone, the role of the conscience is to tell a man whether he is in a state of grace.[57] The conscience is to bear witness whether the believer is trusting in God more than anything else.[58] Though the conscience may be dulled or

---

52 "Church's Riches," in *Works*, 4:517.
53 "Bowels Opened," in *Works*, 2:50; "First Chapter 2 Corinthians," in *Works*, 3:222; cf. John Ball, *Treatise of Faith* (London: 1632), 95.
54 "First Chapter 2 Corinthians," in *Works*, 3:219; cf. 219–21.
55 "First Chapter 2 Corinthians," in *Works*, 227; cf. Calvin, *Institutes*, 3.14.7.
56 "First Chapter 2 Corinthians," in *Works*, 228; cf. Calvin, *Institutes*, 3.14.18.
57 "Demand," in *Works*, 7:486; "First Chapter 2 Corinthians," in *Works*, 3:207.
58 "Faithful Covenanter," in *Works*, 6:11.

suppressed in this life, it is never finally satisfied until God is satisfied.[59] Thus, only as the Holy Spirit quiets the conscience can the believer have the assurance of God's love.[60] Without such a conscience, no certain hope of salvation and heaven can be had.[61]

How the Conscience Is Awakened

Sibbes frequently urged his hearers to labor to have and know a good conscience.[62] How is the believer to wake a naturally sluggish conscience? The more obvious means are prayer, fellowship, preaching, and reflection. Sibbes taught that "sore eyes cannot endure the light; and a galled conscience cannot endure God's presence. Therefore it is good to come oft into the presence of God."[63] Whether individually[64] or corporately, listening to God's Word preached,[65] especially in a searching fashion,[66] awakens the conscience. Yet believers are also to stir the conscience particularly by considering the judgments of God on themselves, on the church abroad, and on the dangers

---

59 "Demand," in *Works*, 7:482.

60 "Angels," in *Works*, 6:352.

61 "Demand," in *Works*, 7:483; cf. Calvin, *Institutes*, 3.13.3; Westminster Confession of Faith 20.1; Westminster Larger Catechism 80.

62 "Demand," in *Works*, 7:489–90; "Divine Meditations," in *Works*, 7:216; "Judgment," in *Works*, 4:90; "Two Sermons," in *Works*, 7:345; "Rich Poverty," in *Works*, 6:261.

63 "Breathing," in *Works*, 2:223.

64 "Bowels Opened," in *Works*, 2:48.

65 "Angels," in *Works*, 6:333.

66 "Soul's Conflict," in *Works*, 1:135.

THE AFFECTIONATE THEOLOGY OF RICHARD SIBBES

in the church at home.[67] Temporal troubles are to be seen as spiritual signs; whenever God opens the conscience by means of particular punishments, it is in order to convict the believer for particular sins, and it is not to be ignored.[68]

Life seemed to confirm to Sibbes that troubles are significant—and the way of understanding them is through attention to the conscience. Therefore, he warned that "he that sleeps with a conscience defiled, is as he that sleeps among wild beasts, among adders and toads, that if his eyes were open to see them, he would be out of his wits."[69] When the conscience is guilty, it magnifies all troubles into God's judgments until the believer heeds the conscience's conviction about the cause.[70] Thus the believer's perception of God's providence in his conscience is to become the ground of his guidance.

CONSCIENCE AS A TOOL OF GROWTH

Sibbes taught that the conscience has more uses as a tool for spiritual growth. The conscience, being sensitive to the wrath of God, is to make a man hate sin and thereby aid his sanctification.[71] Likewise, the conscience keeps the Christian humble

---

67 "Judgment," in *Works*, 4:90; "Divine Meditations," in *Works*, 7:201; "Soul's Conflict," in *Works*, 1:150; cf. Calvin, *Institutes*, 3.2.20.

68 "Bowels Opened," in *Works*, 2:60–61.

69 "First Chapter 2 Corinthians," in *Works*, 3:226.

70 "Bruised Reed," in *Works*, 1:46, 90.

71 "Christ's Suffering," in *Works*, 1:360; "Church's Visitation," in *Works*, 1:375; "Excellency," in *Works*, 4:254.

by showing him his sinfulness, and by recalling particular sins for correction.[72]

However, restoring quietness after sin to the conscience may prove difficult. Time,[73] and even private confession to ministers, Sibbes said, will sometimes be part of quieting the conscience.[74] Through controlling the peace and comfort of a believer, the conscience also acts as a guide, showing how to serve God according to his will and command. Sibbes preached that a good conscience comes not from perfect obedience but from a sincere heart laboring to obey the gospel and keep the covenant with God.[75]

The conscience is to be kept by taking counsel of God in His Word and by binding one's conscience to closer obedience[76]—though often God also "awakens the consciences of his children, and exerciseth them with spiritual conflicts" and even temporary desertions.[77]

72 "Divine Meditations," in *Works*, 7:201; "Returning Backslider," in *Works*, 2:262; "Ungodly's Misery," in *Works*, 1:387; "Faithful Covenanter," in *Works*, 6:16; "Two Sermons," in *Works*, 7:346.
73 "Knot of Prayer," in *Works*, 7:242; "Saint's Hiding-Place," in *Works*, 1:416.
74 "Returning Backslider," in *Works*, 2:261; cf. "Bruised Reed," in *Works*, 1:54.
75 "Demand," in *Works*, 7:490; "First Chapter 2 Corinthians," in *Works*, 3:204–5, 223. Cf. Calvin: "A good conscience, then, is nothing but inward integrity of heart" (*Institutes*, 3.19.1b; cf. 4.10.4).
76 "Privileges," in *Works*, 5:278; "Demand," in *Works*, 7:490–91.
77 "Saint's Safety," in *Works*, 1:316.

BENEFITS OF A GOOD CONSCIENCE

The maintenance of a good conscience is so important to the Christian that Sibbes referred to it as "a heaven on earth . . . the paradise of a good conscience,"[78] encouraging hearers not to be driven out of it as Adam and Eve were from Eden. Since it is the answer to the Holy Spirit's effectual call, Christians begin their new lives with a purified and pacified conscience.[79] If it is kept, the benefits of a good conscience are great: it is easily troubled for sin by the Spirit, easily pacified by the promises of grace, and easily restored to a gracious desire to please God in all things.[80] "When the conscience is clear . . . there is nothing between God and us to hinder our trust."[81] The believer can then be assured that his prayers will be answered[82] and live courageously and with joy, certain of his master's approval.[83] Without such a good conscience, even the stoutest man in the world is a slave.[84]

Finally, one conquers only by having an upright conscience[85]—for only a good conscience can bring true comfort:[86]

---

78 "Danger," in *Works*, 7:410; "Soul's Conflict" in *Works*, 1:134; "First Chapter 2 Corinthians," in *Works*, 3:215–16, 218.

79 "Bride's Longing," in *Works*, 6:541; "Demand," in *Works*, 7:485, 489–90.

80 "Demand," in *Works*, 7:484; "Fountain Opened," in *Works*, 5:493.

81 "Soul's Conflict," in *Works*, 1:241.

82 "Demand," in *Works*, 7:483; cf. Calvin, *Institutes*, 1.20.10, 12.

83 "Excellency," in *Works*, 4:237; "Faithful Covenanter," in *Works*, 6:16; "First Chapter 2 Corinthians," in *Works*, 3:206–7, 223.

84 "Excellency," in *Works*, 4:237; "Soul's Conflict," in *Works*, 1:228.

85 "Divine Meditations," in *Works*, 7:207; "Saint's Safety," in *Works*, 1:322.

86 "Demand," in *Works*, 7:490–91; "Divine Meditations," in *Works*, 7:216; "Rich

In sickness, when a man can eat nothing, a good 'conscience is a continual feast,' Prov. xv.15. In sorrow it is a musician. A good conscience doth not only counsel and advise, but it is a musician to delight. . . . If a man's conscience be wounded, if it be not quieted by faith in the blood of Christ; if he have not the Spirit to witness the forgiveness of his sins, and to sanctify and enable him to lead a good life, all is to no purpose, if there be an evil conscience. The unsound body while it is sick, it is in a kind of hell already.[87]

A good conscience arms the believer against all discouragements,[88] allowing him to "look God in the face"[89]—even being mollified by God when it would threaten for sins already forgiven.[90] In the end, those who have kept a good conscience are truly wise,[91] truly rich[92] people. It follows quite naturally for Sibbes to exclaim:

If it be so, that we cannot do anything nor suffer anything as we should, that we cannot praise God, that

---

Poverty," in *Works*, 6:261; "Yea and Amen," in *Works*, 4:130; "First Chapter 2 Corinthians," in *Works*, 3:215–16. Cf. Calvin, *Institutes*, 3.14.18.

87 "First Chapter 2 Corinthians," in *Works*, 3:217.

88 "Faithful Covenanter," in *Works*, 6:16.

89 "Demand," in *Works*, 7:490. Cf. other related visual imagery in "Angels," in *Works*, 6:333; "Christ's Suffering," in *Works*, 1:357–58; "Demand," in *Works*, 7:486; "Divine Meditations," in *Works*, 7:194.

90 "Rich Pearl," in *Works*, 7:256.

91 "Demand," in *Works*, 7:490–91; "Soul's Conflict," in *Works*, 1:145.

92 "Rich Pearl," in *Works*, 7:259.

we cannot live nor die without joy, and the ground of it, the testimony of a good conscience; let us labour, then, that conscience may witness well unto us.[93]

Therefore how much should we prize and value the testimony and witness of a good conscience! . . . Of all persons and all things in the world, we should reverence our own conscience most of all.[94]

WHEN CONSCIENCE CONFLICTS

Just as the Reformers had been critical of the Roman church's binding of conscience where the gospel had left men free, so too, this issue was a recurring source of dispute in the English church. Though this concern was rarely met explicitly in Sibbes' sermons, it was present implicitly in his frequent exhortations to heed conscience's dictates above the counsels of men.

One can see in Sibbes' pastoral writings—though often explicitly pleading for religious Conformity—the ground of Nonconformity, religious and civil. In September 1631, Sibbes preached in Gray's Inn Chapel, encouraging listeners to part with "riches, pleasures, and honours, life, world . . . for conscience' sake."[95] Words reminiscent of Jesus' in Matthew

---

93 "First Chapter 2 Corinthians," in *Works*, 3:223; cf. 228.
94 "First Chapter 2 Corinthians," in *Works*, 219.
95 "Rich Pearl," in *Works*, 7:259.

19:29 might be preached at any time by a popular preacher; in 1631, however, such words may have had special import to Sibbes' hearers. To the godly, signs of God's judgment seemed imminent, not least in the church: from the godly leaving England because of Laud's innovations to the making of illegal soap (because of objections to the Crown's giving soap money to the Queen's Roman Catholic friends), godly consciences were being heeded.[96]

Conscience is to be treated as above all things other than God[97] because "conscience is above me and above all men in the world"[98] and should be revered even "more than any monarch in the world."[99] Therefore, "every man is to follow most what his own conscience, after information, dictates unto him; because conscience is God's deputy in us, and under God most to be regarded, and whosoever sins against it, in his own construction sins against God."[100]

It is important to note an important caveat in Sibbes' teaching on conscience. Though Sibbes taught that the conscience is the moral guardian in the soul, and that it is perilous to ignore it, he did not suggest that the conscience is always

---

96 Robert Ashton, *The City and the Court, 1603–1643* (Cambridge, England: Cambridge University Press, 1979), 141–43.

97 "Excellency," in *Works*, 4:220; cf. "Angels," in *Works*, 6:352.

98 "First Chapter 2 Corinthians," in *Works*, 3:210.

99 "First Chapter 2 Corinthians," in *Works*, 3:225; cf. 500; Calvin, *Institutes*, 3.19.14–15; 4.10.4, 8; Perkins, *Galatians*, 325–26, 361–62.

100 "Soul's Conflict," in *Works*, 1:211; cf. "First Chapter 2 Corinthians," in *Works*, 3:211.

right.[101] Indeed, he specifically denied this,[102] teaching that, since conscience can be misled, one can and should work to educate the conscience—primarily through the Word, but also through the implications of the two tables of the law worked out (fallibly) by the church and the state.[103] Thus, conscience is not the ground of Nonconformity, but the avenue to Conformity: "It will be the heaviest sin that can be laid to our charge at the day of judgment, not that we were ignorant, but that we refused to know, we refused to have our conscience rectified and instructed."[104]

Unlike the Word itself, both the church and the civil law are open to abuse as avenues of education. While both are to instruct the conscience, neither should follow the example of the Roman church by attempting to usurp the place of the

---

101 "In the Reformers' use of the term 'conscience,' the static condition of an inclination to good is completely dispelled by the reality of man's inclination to evil, which is experienced with fear, as the divine law is used by the Holy Spirit to tear away man's pretensions," (G.C. Berkouwer, *Man: The Image of God*, trans. D. Jellema [Grand Rapids, Mich.: 1962], 172).

102 "First Chapter 2 Corinthians," in *Works*, 3:219. "The judgments of the individual conscience are as much subject to argument and correction as any other intellectual proposition; they are not immune to criticism as if based on an inward and private apprehension of God's will," (Conrad Wright, "John Cotton Washed and Made White," in *Continuity and Discontinuity in Church History*, eds. T.T. Church and F. George, [Leiden, Netherlands: Brill, 1979], 342).

103 "Soul's Conflict," in *Works*, 1:211; "Angels," in *Works*, 6:329; "Divine Meditations," in *Works*, 7:201; "First Chapter 2 Corinthians," in *Works*, 3:209, 213–14, 374. Cf. Bernard Verkamp, *The Indifferent Mean: Adiaphorism in the English Reformation to 1554* (Athens, Ohio: Ohio University Press, 1977), 9; Yule, 16–25.

104 "First Chapter 2 Corinthians," in *Works*, 3:213; cf. "The Unprosperous Builder," in *Works*, 7:31; "Excellency," in *Works*, 4:257–58; "Judgment," in *Works*, 4:110.

conscience.[105] In his popular sermons *The Soul's Conflict with Itself*, Sibbes told his hearers at Gray's Inn:

> We must look to our place wherein God hath set us. If we be in subjection to others, their authority *in doubtful things ought to sway with us. It is certain we ought to obey; and if the thing wherein we are to obey be uncertain unto us, we ought to leave that which is uncertain and stick to that which is certain; in this case we must obey those that are gods under God.* Neither is it the calling for those that are subjects, to inquire over curiously into the mysteries of government; for that, both in peace and war, breeds much disturbance, and would trouble all designs. The laws under which we live are particular determinations of the law of God in some duties of the second table. . . . Where it dashes not against God's law, what is agreeable to law is agreeable to conscience. [emphasis added][106]

To discover what Sibbes thought to be the essence of the church theologically—godly preaching, right administration of the sacraments, some discipline—is to discover what

---

105 "Bowels Opened," in *Works*, 2:120; "First Chapter 2 Corinthians," in *Works*, 3:214, 500–504; "Unprosperous Builder," in *Works*, 7:24. Cf. Calvin, *Reply*, 243; Calvin, *Romans*, 283; Verkamp, 9–54. Sibbes' insistence on the authority of the conscience should be seen in the light of a growing number of adiaphorous matters being advocated as part of the faith in the English church.

106 "Soul's Conflict," in *Works*, 1:209–10.

Sibbes thought to be essential to the church practically (and by implication, those things that were nonessential).[107] Divisions caused in the church, for reasons other than essential matters, Sibbes relegated to divisions for "private aims," even if the divider was right on the particular, he was wrong to cause division about anything not "necessary."[108]

Though he did not consider the Elizabethan Settlement perfect, Sibbes felt it should be left to those to whom it had been entrusted to govern the church.[109] Furthermore, the cause of much unnecessary division was a lack of faith in God's future provision based on His promises, a childish peevishness that, "when they have not what they would have, like children, they throw all away."[110] Such childishness, combined with ignorance of true Christian liberty, led to unnecessary scruples. Instead of despairing separation, Sibbes said that one should have faith because "faith makes things to come present."[111]

Sibbes' own experience in the church had encouraged his willingness and strengthened his ability to see with the eye of faith, trusting that good things, unseen at the time, were yet coming. "Look with other spectacles, with the eye of faith,

---

107 "Consolatory Letter," in *Works*, 1:lxxiii–cxvi; cf. "Church's Visitation," in *Works*, 1:375–76.

108 "Bruised Reed," in *Works*, 1:76.

109 "If there had been a thorough reformation in the church after her former trouble, and a thorough closing with Christ, she would not thus have fallen into a more dangerous condition," ("Bowels Opened," in *Works*, 2:38).

110 "Soul's Conflict," in *Works*, 1:136.

111 "First Chapter 2 Corinthians," in *Works*, 3:93.

and then you shall see a spring in the winter of the church."[112] Just as the true believer could be assured of his destination by the authenticity of his present experience, so the corrupt church, Sibbes believed, if authentic, could be sure of God's ultimate and complete sanctification and vindication—perhaps uncertain of the means, but not the end.[113] Therefore, "in some cases peace . . . is of more consequence than the open discovery of some things we take to be true . . . open show of difference is never good but when it is necessary."[114] While some "for a little smoke will quench the light; Christ ever we see cherisheth even the least beginnings."[115] Sibbes concluded, "I had rather hazard the censure of some, than hinder the good of others."[116]

If the choice of Conformity had been difficult for Sibbes' conscience in 1616, it could hardly have been less so in 1633, when a number of those close to Sibbes decided that they could no longer conscientiously conform. Yet, however disturbed he may have been at the ill signs for the future of the Reformed church in England, Sibbes' conscience was educated—aided not only by Sibbes' "eye of faith" but also by his belief in providence.

112 "Fountain Opened," in *Works*, 5:491; cf. "Bowels Opened," in *Works*, 2:136, 180; "Church's Visitation," in *Works*, 1:375; Preston, *Breast-Plate*, pt. i, 113; Stoever, 159.

113 "Bowels Opened," in *Works*, 2:85, 23; "Soul's Conflict," in *Works*, 1:209, 225, 244, 262; "Saint's Safety," in *Works*, 1:312, 318.

114 "Bruised Reed," in *Works*, 1:76.

115 "Bruised Reed," in *Works*, 1:51.

116 "Bruised Reed," in *Works*, 1:41; cf. 55.

After the plague was particularly severe in Cambridge in 1630, Sibbes preached that God "hath given us our lives more than once, every one of us in particularly especially in regard of the last heavy visitation."[117] God is active in history; His people were to be "warned by public dangers."[118] It was only "worldly, sottish men that live here below, they think there is no other state of things than they see; they are only taken up with sense, and pleasures, and goodly shows of things. Alas! poor souls!"[119] But Christians should use such providential happenings to awaken their consciences.[120] Even as in Acts 5 God had judged His enemies and delivered His church from their deceit, so He would ultimately provide revenge for his enemies and salvation for His church.[121] Observing God's providence can prepare His people, "we know not what times God may call us to ere long."[122] Through such observations, God's faithfulness can be discerned and the believer's faith strengthened.

---

117 "Saint's Safety," in *Works*, 1:311.

118 "Demand," in *Works*, 7:491; cf. "Bowels Opened," in *Works*, 2:43, 65–67; "Divine Meditations," in *Works*, 7:208; "Fountain Opened," in *Works*, 5:512; "Soul's Conflict," in *Works*, 1:197, 204–6, 210, 231, 244; "Privileges," in *Works*, 5:269; and, of course, "Providence," in *Works*, 5:35–54; Miller, *Mind*, 38–40; Keith Thomas, *Religion and the Decline of Magic* (London: Penguin, 1971), 90–132.

119 "Angels," in *Works*, 6:319.

120 "Judgment," in *Works*, 4:90.

121 Sibbes allowed that God's government of the church was more "outward in the primitive times of the church ("Judgment," in *Works*, 4:83).

122 "Art," in *Works*, 5:193; cf. "Bowels Opened," in *Works*, 2:181; "Danger," in *Works*, 7:412; "Fountain Opened," in *Works*, 5:466; "Judgment," in *Works*, 4:95; "Saint's Hiding-Place," in *Works*, 1:425.

Yet, Sibbes taught, it is not the reading of God's providence but relying on God's promises that should ultimately strengthen the believer's faith and instruct his conscience. Informed by his own experience of fruitful ministry within the church, and aided by the gradualism that typified his understanding of the action of God's grace in conviction, conversion, comfort, and assurance within the covenant community, Sibbes conscientiously conformed. In Sibbes, the inward piety of comfort, assurance, and the conscience was tied up closely with the fallible, visible church, regardless of whether it needed to be. For Sibbes, this inward piety was not the avenue to Nonconformity, but what allowed continuing Conformity.

Sibbes also referred to an "inbred light in the soul" and an "infused establishing by the Spirit," both of which were intelligences gained apart from the senses.[123] This understanding of the nature of conscience led to Sibbes' other conflicting emphasis on accountability to conscience alone, under God, and gave to conscience such authority that it was never to be dismissed—though it could not save, it must be heeded; though it needed instruction, it could not be ignored.[124] It was this equivocation that aided Sibbes' representation in the eighteenth century as a Nonconformist, despite his actual Conformity. While there is no dispute that Sibbes taught that, "where it [law] dashes not against God's law, what is agreeable

---

123 "First Chapter 2 Corinthians," in *Works*, 3:427; cf. 260.
124 "Glance of Heaven," in *Works*, 4:159; cf. Breward, 33.

to law is agreeable to conscience," this was merely a statement of what should be. The years after Sibbes' death revealed the profound conflicts that could emerge between the obligations of humbly educating one's conscience on one hand, and on the other, heeding it at all costs.

The Significance of Sibbes for Puritan Studies

Almost four centuries after his death, Richard Sibbes continues to be a celebrated Puritan. For almost thirty years at this writing, the nineteenth-century edition of his collected works has remained in print, lining the shelves of Anglican, Reformed, and evangelical ministers. Yet, between the vast tract of those lost to history and those few who have been the subject of painstaking study, Sibbes has inhabited an academic no-man's land marked by the combination of ignorance and prominence. Known by inclusion in short lists and citations of apt sayings, he is a man wrested from obscurity, deserving the privilege of a thorough study.

The mists of history have enclosed Sibbes so as to render him historically invisible or, at least, indistinct. He has suffered from being accurately, yet partially, described on scores of issues, with the result that he has been a widely mistaken character; other representations have been even less accurate on the particulars. Given both the nature and number of his writings extant, almost any casual interpretation of him and his theology can be sustained.

The goal of this study has been to recover Sibbes as a historical and theological whole. Most of the study's sources have been printed, and its subject well known. Though Sibbes was popular, even celebrated, during his life, his thought could hardly be said to have been seminal, nor his career determinative for the fortunes of the godly in early Stuart England. Yet the disadvantage of the limited extent to this study, which has focused on Sibbes alone, may be offset by the resulting care that can be given to specifics. While there remains much work to do on Sibbes, this volume has attempted to present him clearly in both his historical and theological contexts.

Contrary to previous presentations, it appears that Sibbes did subscribe to the three articles and conform. There is no reason to believe that he was deprived of his lectureship at Holy Trinity, Cambridge, and it is certain that he was not put out of his fellowship at St. John's. Nor should Sibbes be seen as a disruptive force in the Anglican Church.

The origin of the great reversal in Sibbes' reputation from a Conforming moderate to a deprived Nonconformist has been briefly noted in chapter two; the development of the myth of Sibbes as a Puritan martyr is full of assumptions innocently presented as fact, with dependence on secondary sources rather than primary ones; yet this image has prevailed. This is understandable given the universally reported deprivations he suffered, but it is surprising that the prevailing view has not previously raised more questions, given Sibbes' subsequent preferment and reputation. The tradition of reporting the history of the Puritan movement as simply the earliest chapter of Dissenting history has remained intact in Sibbes' case, to the detriment of an accurate portrayal. Thanks to their inclusion in two standard reference works often cited by later historians—James Venn's *Alumni Cantabrigienses* and Alexander Gordon's article on Sibbes in the *Dictionary of National Biography*—the errors surrounding Sibbes and his leaving Cambridge for London were joined together and canonized, becoming biographical "facts" about Richard Sibbes. The normal course for historical writers since has been to repeat the story of Sibbes' deprivation, almost whenever his name is mentioned.

Sibbes' move from Cambridge to London in 1617 is much more likely explained by his talent for fostering friendships, combined with his obvious gifts as a preacher. His skill at making and retaining friendships helps at least to account for his successful involvement with the Feoffees (before their dissolution), his successful mastership of Katharine Hall, and perhaps for much more. They do not, however, suggest any religious radicalism that would encourage separation. This is clearly ruled out, not only negatively by the weakness of the argument itself, but also by noting Sibbes' explicit defenses of the Church of England, together with the general tone of his writing and career.

Yet as that which Sibbes took quite literally to be the salvation of the Church of England—godly preaching—became increasingly hindered by those in authority, his own position in the church certainly appeared more incongruous. However, his faithful adherence to the Church of England was consistent with his own experience and theology. His experience of authority was not almost wholly negative, as one might assume from earlier presentations; rather, Sibbes knew the benefits of wealthy patrons. He often experienced help from those in authority, which is perhaps why he was able to continue to trust a hierarchy that was turning against what he recognized as the very means of grace.

Sibbes' loyalty to the Church of England was also consistent with his theology. He understood the church to be a covenant community far more extensive than the elect, intended to be filled with people in various spiritual states. Therefore, imperfection was expected and tolerated—though not excused—and the use of means vigorously encouraged. Indeed, the covenant obliged one to live a life of holiness. Sibbes' interiorization of piety—not unique to him, but powerfully communicated in his sermons—accounts for his popularity with disparate groups, for his ability to conform to the demands of the church, and also for the potential for a Christianity lived in disobedience to ungodly earthly authorities. Sibbes was not a mere moralist; he understood the church to be a supernatural, sovereign creation of God. The theology of God's sovereignty was not eclipsed by Sibbes' use of covenant terminology, nor by any of his exhortations to the use of means—nor was the ultimate accountability of the individual before God eclipsed by his affirmation of the need to educate one's conscience. Sibbes clearly taught that only the ultimate authority was fully trustworthy, and full trustworthiness always characterized the ultimate authority, God.

That Sibbes was able to remain within the Church of England until his death in 1635 should not, however, be used to suggest that his Conformity appeared uniform throughout his life, nor that he was as representative of the church in 1635 as he may have been a quarter of a century earlier. Whereas in his early days as a fellow of St. John's, Sibbes may well have been typical of even the majority of the religious types in his college and university, by his last two years he was a noted representative of an important, though shrinking and aging, group of moderate Puritans within the church. This is not too puzzling: just as the deprivations he did not suffer were long taken to be the natural expression of a Separatist ecclesiology he did not hold, so the Conformity he embraced initially was the natural expression of his own experience and beliefs.

If this study has been historically helpful in representing Sibbes more accurately as one of a growing number of moderate Puritans in the early seventeenth-century Church of England, it can be most helpful theologically in suggesting some shortcomings in assuming that the covenant framework somehow undermined the bases of Reformed theology. Both drawing on earlier observations, but independently of each other, Perry Miller and Karl Barth suggested that this undermining had occurred. Though the two men and their concerns could hardly have been more different—Miller was a confidently atheistic American historian, and Barth a devout Swiss Reformed theologian—they came to strikingly similar conclusions about the effects of covenant theology on Reformed thought. Miller's optimistic rationalism left him puzzled by the Reformed roots of New England; looking back at Calvin, and disliking what he took to be the irrationalism he saw, Miller observed a growing reliance on and confidence in reason in Calvin's later heirs, particularly among the covenant theologians. Barth, on the other hand, as an unabashed champion of Calvin, saw in the more explicit covenant formulations that followed a creeping anthropocentrism that obscured grace. Though Miller in particular has influenced later theological interpretations of seventeenth-century Puritanism, it was the powerful combination of these concerns by church historians such as Basil Hall and J.B. Torrance that gave them particular weight with other historians, who were ready to cede all knowledge of things theological to experts trained in that field.

The most influential recent study to reinvigorate debate on this issue was R.T. Kendall's *Calvin and English Calvinism to 1649*. Though this work is widely quoted as theologically authoritative by recent historians, it is marked by several flaws, some of which are addressed in this book. If one of the advantages of studies like Miller's and Kendall's is that they can be helpful in digesting, summarizing, and organizing information, one of the disadvantages is the potential for ignorance of particulars and slighting of specifics. In particular, Kendall's drawing of comparisons between figures from different eras and situations—a difficult, but needful, task—is rendered less helpful than it appears thanks to his scant attention to the historical setting. Kendall's analysis becomes, in fact, misleading, as Calvin's statements, which were uttered in the context of polemic against the form of Christianity all around him and ever-beckoning to the inhabitants of Geneva, are put "in conversation" with statements made by English preachers fifty and a hundred years later in a national Protestant church.

In 1697, John Higginson, 81-year-old minister of the church in Salem, Mass., looked back on the first generation of ministers (which included his father) who came from England to New England, remarking, "Our fathers did in their time acknowledge, there were many defects and imperfections in our way, and yet we believe they did as much as could be expected from learned and godly men in their circumstances."[1] Such was the respect accorded Sibbes by those after his death who differed from him, yet esteemed him. To Richard Baxter, Sibbes was one of those "old moderate sort" of

---

1   John Higginson, "An Attestation to the Church-History," prefixed to Cotton
     Mather, *Magnalia Christi Americana* (Hartford, Conn.: 1853), 1:17.

"Episcopal men . . . who were commonly in Doctrine Calvinists."[2] Not that Sibbes was a moderate man when preaching of the necessity of justification by faith, the certainty of God's salvation of the elect, or the duty of all members of the covenant to fulfill their obligations. His moderation was reserved for those externals of religion, which he deemed matters of indifference and which his church deemed edifying—the sign of the cross, the use of clerical garments, and perhaps even an unworthy recipient of a fellowship. Even in his last years when he must have felt most circumscribed and could have most easily despaired, he remained a member of "the sacred communion of the truly Evangelicall Church of England."[3] Reflecting a lifetime of fruitful experience, it is understandable that in his will Sibbes should commend his soul to God "with humble thankes that he hath vouchsafed I should be borne and live in the best tymes of the gospell."[4]

---

2   Richard Baxter, *Reliquae Baxterianae*, ed. Matthew Sylvester (London: 1696), ii.149.

3   "Consolatory Letter," in *Works*, 1:cxvi.

4   "David's Epitaph," in *Works*, 6:495.

INDEX

ABOUT THE AUTHOR

Dr. Mark Dever serves as senior pastor of Capitol Hill Baptist Church in Washington, D.C., and president of 9Marks Ministries. He is a graduate of Duke University and holds an M.Div. from Gordon-Conwell Theological Seminary, a Th.M. from The Southern Baptist Theological Seminary, and a Ph.D. in ecclesiastical history from Cambridge University. He has taught at a number of seminaries and is a frequent conference speaker.

Dr. Dever has authored or coauthored several books and articles, including his most recent, *Discipling: How to Help Others Follow Jesus*, *The Compelling Community: Where God's Power Makes a Church Attractive* (with Jamie Dunlop), and *The Church: The Gospel Made Visible*. Earlier books include *What Is a Healthy Church?*, *The Gospel and Personal Evangelism*, *Nine Marks of a Healthy Church*, *The Deliberate Church*, *Promises Kept: The Message of the New Testament*, and *Promises Made: The Message of the Old Testament*.

He and his wife, Connie, live and minister on Capitol Hill, with Connie giving much of her time to creating a children's curriculum. They have two adult children.